Choosing
the
Amusing

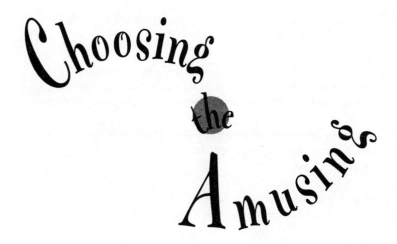

Choosing the Amusing

Marilyn Meberg

WORD PUBLISHING

NASHVILLE

A Thomas Nelson Company

Unless otherwise indicated, all scripture references are from the New American Standard Bible, ©The Lockman Foundation 1960, 1962, 1963, 1968, 1971, 1972, 1973, 1975, 1977. Used by permission.

Scripture references marked NIV are from the Holy Bible: New International Version, copyright 1978 by the International Bible Society. Used by permission of Zondervan Bible Publishers.

"Dream Deferred" from *Collected Poems* by Langston Hughes. Copyright ©1994 by the Estate of Langston Hughes. Reprinted by permission of Alfred A. Knopf Inc.

First published in 1986 by Multnomah Press

Library of Congress Cataloging-in-Publication Data
Meberg, Marilyn.
    Choosing the amusing.
    1. Christian life—1960–   . 2. Wit and humor—Religious aspects—Christianity.
    3. Meberg, Marilyn.
    ISBN 0-8499-3744-2
    I. Title
    BV4501.2.M442   1986
    248.4
                                                            85-32071

Printed in the United States of America
99 00 01 02 03 04 05 06 QPV 9 8 7 6 5 4 3 2 1

To my father, Jasper Ricker, whose
quick wit and keen appreciation of
the laughable has instructed me
well in choosing the amusing.

Contents

Part 1: Why We Should Laugh

Part 2: Why We Don't Laugh

Foreword

Of all the things God created, I am often most grateful that he created laughter. How I love to have fun! In all honesty, I can hardly imagine a day spent without at least a few moments (preferably many) of sidesplitting laughter . . . either alone or with someone who can enjoy them as much as I. What healing it brings to our heavy hearts! Abe Lincoln's sentiments are mine as well: "With the fearful strain that is on me night and day, if I did not laugh, I should die." Who can measure the oil it adds to our otherwise dry internal gears? The relief it brings to our weary bones is undeniable.

Folks who enjoy life's lighter side help me stay balanced and sane in a world that seems overrun with intense, tight-lipped souls who spend their lives grimly awaiting the drop of the other shoe. And since humor is such a vital tool in my survival kit, I tend to gravitate toward those who are relaxed enough to laugh at and with life . . . which explains my longtime friendship with Marilyn Meberg.

My wife, Cynthia, and I met the Meberg family in the spring of 1971, and we have been laughing together ever since. Marilyn's remarkable ability to discover the humor in everyday situations is equaled only by her creative skill to describe it to others. As you will soon discover, this is one hilarious lady. But that is not to say that she is shallow or superficial.

On the contrary, Marilyn is a captivating conversationalist, a deep-thinking, multitalented person whose world is broad and whose roles are numerous, including wife, mother, educator, speaker, and author. While she has not been shielded from life's dark and difficult times, she has certainly not lost her zest, a quality I appreciate the most about her. As a matter of fact, her positive optimism has passed all tests with flying colors.

Therefore, it is with much delight and with loud applause that I commend *Choosing the Amusing* to you. It will make you think, which is good for you. And it will make you laugh, which is even better. So don't hold back! Fred Allen used to say that it was bad to suppress laughter because it goes back down and spreads your hips. That alone is enough to keep all of us loose!

Here is a book to enjoy, so sit back, relax, and enjoy it. Nothing would make Marilyn Meberg happier . . . except, perhaps, your buying a big stack of them for your friends to enjoy with you.

Chuck Swindoll

Special Note to Reader

M any things have changed in my life since 1986 when *Choosing the Amusing* was first published. My two children are now happily married and Ken has gone to be with the Lord. One thing, however, has not changed and that is the biblical wisdom of Proverbs 17:22 from which this book receives its inspiration.

I am delighted to see *Choosing the Amusing* come back into print and welcome you to its exploration of how and why choosing the amusing is a lifestyle worth pursuing.

May your spirit be lifted and your health soar as you embrace the truth that "a joyful heart is good medicine."

Proposing a Laugh Lifestyle

Artemus Ward, the nineteenth-century American humorist, wrote: "It would have been ten dollars in that guy's pocket if he had never been born." That statement gives you momentary whiplash until the meaning as well as the humor becomes clear. On a bleak day some of us may identify with the illogical logic of Ward's comment as we think, *For ten dollars I'd volunteer not to be born—in fact, I'd volunteer not to be born for free!* Some days just don't seem to be worth it.

Charlie Brown, the lovable cartoon character, says: "I've developed a new philosophy. . . . I only dread one day at a time." We smile indulgently at Charlie Brown, the hapless victim of his environment, and yet I wonder if there are not many Charlie Browns in the world who quietly live their lives in dread of the next day—perhaps wishing they had volunteered not to be born. These thoughts and feelings obviously do not reflect a joyful or optimistic spirit. They come from persons in need of a little medicine. God says in Proverbs 17:22, "A joyful heart is good medicine, but a broken spirit dries up the bones." God prescribes a joyful heart as the medicine we need to combat the broken spirits and dry bones that cause us to live our days in quiet dread.

That sounds like a great prescription, but how do we take our medicine and experience joyful hearts? I propose that laughter is a potent, healing, and rejuvenating contribution to our joy. We all love to laugh and even wish we laughed more, but some of us have lost our inclination because our joy lies buried in the rubble of broken spirits and dry bones.

In part 1 of this book I'd like to challenge you to see the emotional, physical, and spiritual value of laughter—to recognize its medicinal importance to our daily living. In part 2 we'll talk about some of those attitudes and mindsets that break our spirits, dry our bones, and bury our laughs. And then in the last chapter we'll talk about how to actually develop a more active "laugh lifestyle."

I have written this book desiring that it will provide some helpful suggestions—and that it will inspire a laugh or two as you read. Maybe you can start filling your prescription in the first chapter. Try it and see!

part
1

Why We
Should Laugh

"*A joyful heart is good medicine.*"

We Are Relaxed

1

One of the richest sources of humor lies within ourselves and our own experiences. Many times, however, we fail to acknowledge or even recognize that source of humor. When we take ourselves and our lives too seriously, we miss opportunities for a good laugh, and the tension this produces can kill future laughs before they are even born. A good laugh can make us relax or "mellow out." Let me cite one of my unnecessarily uptight responses to motherhood when my son, Jeff, was eighteen months old.

Jeff was hopelessly addicted to his pacifier. This concerned me because he looked mildly moronic with that rubber plug perpetually hanging out of his mouth, and he smelled bad as well. The rubber literally began to rot from constant use, and the smell of its decay clung to Jeff wherever he went.

The obvious solution of providing a new pacifier didn't work because he flatly refused any contact with one. I thought, *Why on earth would anyone in their right mind refuse a brand-new, inoffensive pacifier when it provides a classier look and a better aroma?*

Clearly this child was not concerned with aesthetics. As the days dragged on, the odor intensified. I became desperate; my desperation produced tension. I studied Jeff as he would "plug in" his rank, little aid-to-peace, turning it slightly in his mouth until he achieved exactly the right feel. Then it hit me. He was attached to the old pacifier because it had ridges that conformed exactly to the contours of his mouth. It was a custom fit! It was familiar—homey—comfortable. The new one was foreign—sterile—stiff. At that moment I determined to form ridges on the new pacifier. There was only one way to do this—I would simply have to break it in myself!

I was well aware of the absurdity of this plan. The picture of a mother so driven by desperation that she would actually do what I was planning to do did amuse me. Nevertheless, in spite of the glimpse of humor I saw, I remained inordinately serious. I even entertained the possibility of Jeff and I developing a deeper level of camaraderie and identification as we went about each day sucking our mutual pacifiers.

On the first morning of this plan's enactment, Jeff settled in to watch *Captain Kangaroo*. As he plugged in, I sat down beside him and also plugged in. It took awhile for him to notice me, but when he did, he was vehement in his response. With a determined "No!" he yanked the pacifier out of my mouth and threw it on the floor. This happened several times; each time I tried to explain that Jeff had his pacifier and Mommy had hers, and we were going to enjoy them together. (Incidentally, there is nothing enjoyable or even pacifying about sucking a pacifier. The little rubber center threatened to activate the gag impulse in me, my mouth became dry and my lips tired from pooching out!) Jeff was unmoved by my explanation. Throughout the day, whenever Jeff saw it in my mouth, he would dash up to me, wrench it from my lips, and throw it on the floor. He skulked about the house in an attempt to catch me "at it." Since my plan distressed Jeff, I determined to take to the pacifier when he was safely put away.

That evening, shortly after Jeff had gone to bed, my husband Ken and I were sitting on the couch reading the paper. He made an interesting comment and I lowered my paper in response. He exhibited the same shock and revulsion to my pacifier-stuffed mouth as Jeff had earlier. Later that night, when I thought Ken was asleep, I reached over to the nightstand and noiselessly slipped the pacifier in my mouth. After a few minutes Ken raised up on an elbow and demanded, "What's that munching sound?" I had no idea I was audibly munching. I was then informed that no man in his right mind would go to bed with a woman who slept with a pacifier.

The number of hours available to me for ridge-development were lessening all the time, but a workable pattern subsequently developed. I simply plugged in during Jeff's morning and afternoon naps, which gave me at least two hours a day to work on my project.

One morning about ten days later, I was vacuuming the living room, pacifier firmly in place. I thought I heard a knock. Without turning off the vacuum, I opened the door a few inches and peeked around it. To my chagrin, there stood a salesman with a satchel full of brushes. As his face registered a look of complete bewilderment, I quickly unplugged both vacuum and pacifier. He had not said a word; he just stared. Seeing him back away, I felt compelled to explain what I was doing.

"Now wait a minute," I said. "I know this looks peculiar but, you see, this pacifier isn't mine! Well, what I mean is . . . it's my little boy's . . . he's asleep right now . . . I only suck on it when he's asleep. It upsets him if I suck on it when he's awake. It upsets my husband, too, for that matter! The only reason I've got this one in my mouth is because the other one got to smelling so bad I couldn't stand it any longer."

He continued staring at me. Just as I was about to launch into the importance of forming ridges and to show him that I was actually about to accomplish my goal, he burst into a fit of raucous laughter. He laughed, gasped, choked, and then laughed some more. I thought, *Well, really! I didn't invite this perfect stranger to my door*

. . . and now, having caught me at a rather awkward moment, he has the audacity to gasp and wheeze in the face of my explanations! When he managed to get his breath, he raised one hand weakly in an almost defensive gesture and said, "Lady, I don't know what you are doing, and I don't care. I just want you to know you've made my day." He then went into another fit of laughter and lurched down the sidewalk toward his parked car. Strangely enough, I haven't seen him again, but it's just as well since I prefer to buy my brushes at the supermarket.

Several days later, without the slightest hesitation, Jeff took the pacifier I had broken in; he never knew what I had done. (I confessed ten years later. Happily, by then he had kicked his habit.)

I was so determined my plan would succeed that I failed to see the humor in my actions. When the brush salesman laughed uproariously at me, I was truly indignant. In fact, it wasn't until I described the whole experience to Ken that night and watched him collapse all over the kitchen drainboard that I realized it really had been a funny scene. Because I was taking my mission so seriously and allowing my uptightness to dictate my responses, I came close to missing a good laugh. Who wouldn't laugh at the sight of a woman with a vacuum cleaner hose in her hand and a pacifier in her mouth?

More often than not, we miss laugh possibilities because we see ourselves and everything that happens to us through a lens that refuses to focus on our own absurdities or the absurdities around us. Instead we feel only the tension those absurdities may create.

For instance, this past weekend I had a peculiar experience that did not seem humorous at all—at first.

I was scheduled to speak at a women's retreat in the mountains near Big Bear, California. My friend Pat Wenger went with me to provide companionship and to drive. (My sensitive and often short-winded Fiat would have refused to navigate anything as arduous as a hairpin curve.) Shortly before arriving at our destination, we stopped at a location that dubiously promised gasoline. There were two securely padlocked gas pumps in front of a little country store and an adjoining restaurant whose sign boasted "Home-cooked food like you never had at home."

We waited for a few minutes while nothing happened. Our time was limited, so I jumped out of the car in search of life. The bubblegum-blowing woman in the country store told me, "The place to get gas is from the cook in the restaurant next door." There was nothing in her face that hinted intentional humor with that remark, so I bit my lip, and went next door to find the gas-producing cook. A young man met me with a hopeful smile and said, "Two for dinner?" Since I was the only one standing there I didn't know if his question reflected poor vision or my need to shed a few pounds. I assumed he had seen the two of us sitting in the car by the unattended gas pumps.

When I asked if we could get gas he told me that the cook could not leave the kitchen because he was slicing roast beef, but he would probably be done in thirty or forty minutes. I couldn't believe it! Feeling the urgency of my time schedule, I said, "You mean I have to wait forty minutes to get gas because the cook has to pump it? Why can't I pump it myself?" This question seemed too great a challenge—he simply walked away, so Pat and I decided to wait it out over a piece of pie. Our pie slices could well have served as Ping-Pong paddles; their claim to home-cooked food like you never had at home was no exaggeration.

After forty minutes we inquired about the progress of the roast-beef slicing. Our waiter informed us that the cook had stepped out to find a plunger because the restroom facility had plugged up. When I heard that, I felt one of my worst spells coming on. Sensing my hostile spirit, the waiter said he had to serve some fried chicken, a tossed salad, and a bowl of rice pudding, and then he'd come out and pump the gas for us.

While we waited in the front seat of Pat's car, a dilapidated vehicle came screeching to a halt several yards from us. The two men in the car were wrestling. It wasn't clear whether they were mad at each other or simply engaging in behavior rarely seen in civilized circles. The passenger door popped open, the two filthy, bearded men fell to the asphalt and continued their wrestling. Apparently they were not angry but simply feeling the effects of their afternoon beverages.

The whole experience was so absurdly out of sync that it gave me whiplash. Here I was sitting in the luxurious comfort of Pat's leather front seat with polished nails, recently colored hair, and the soft scent of French perfume, watching two drunken cavemen frolic while our waiter, who had dried Thousand Island dressing on his forearm, pumped our gas in place of the cook, who was somewhere scrounging up a plunger. As we drove off, the craziness of it all began to settle on us. We started to laugh and the farther we drove, the harder we laughed! I had felt increasing tension and irritation as this scene was unfolding, but the outrageous humor of it soon diminished my tension until now, five days later, I think it was probably the highlight of the weekend.

Wouldn't it have been good, though, if I had been able to enter into the humor of that experience sooner than I did? I could have saved myself an elevation in blood pressure—but I didn't because of my self-absorption and concentration on the task at hand.

I believe the potential as well as the need for laughter extends beyond our individual preoccupations to the broader concerns of the world. Leo Buscaglia wrote an interesting newspaper article in which he asked, "What is wrong with people today? Nobody ever laughs!" He went on to say:

> You know, I've got a private fantasy. This fantasy is that instead of all the pompous rulers of the world coming together to talk about disarmament and economy, why don't we send our humorists? Every single country

send[s] their best comedian. Get them together and let them laugh about the problems of the world! It would be a nice switch! A good break. Laughter is a universal language. Let everybody laugh a little bit. Some of the leaders I don't think know how.[1]

I love Buscaglia's statement that laughter is a universal language. A hearty, international laugh that transcends the barriers of language, culture, and politics could be a great tension breaker. Of course there is nothing funny about nuclear war, starvation, or human oppression. But we need periodic release from the obligation to be serious about life's responsibilities. If we can laugh occasionally, we can experience a respite from the burdensome cares and pressures of human existence. The pressures may not go away, but we can possibly view them with less tension. When our tension is relieved, we can get back to the serious business which occupies the majority of our time, and we return with a more relaxed spirit.

The late President John F. Kennedy believed in the value of laughter as a tension reliever. In the middle of the Cuban missile crisis, he was introduced to Bob Basso, who now runs a company called Laughter Therapy. Basso was then a navy lieutenant. As the president was preparing to meet with a group of advisors, he turned to Basso and said, "Lieutenant Basso, tell me a joke." Though Basso considered it an unusual time for joke telling, he did as the president requested. Kennedy apparently liked the joke and said he planned to use it to open the meeting. He later told Basso that humor was his greatest source of relieving tension; he said he doubted his ability to keep a balanced perspective without it.

What I am advocating here is not a mindless giggling through the serious events that touch our lives. Whether it is on a global, national, or personal level, I am suggesting that humor is often overlooked as an invaluable tension reliever. I believe we all have a tremendous potential to laugh, to see the humor in ourselves and in our experiences. I use the word *potential* because many of us have yet to realize our potential for humor. We frequently hear statements like, "Oh yes, he has a great sense of humor" or "She is so funny—I love to be around her" as if these favored few were unique and set apart by their capacity to create or appreciate humor. I believe we all have the capacity for fun and laughter. We do not all have the same abilities in creating humor—we are not all stand-up comics, but we can all laugh. Many of us, however, need to be released from the bondage of our circumstances and ourselves so that the inherent capacity to laugh, which lives in us all, can bubble to the surface and carry us through those times that are tension producing and spirit breaking.

We Are in Control

Theodore S. Geisel, writer of scores of children's books and better known as Dr. Suess, has charmed both children and adults with his delightful depiction of a world in which characters and events are exaggeratedly unusual and out of step with the ordinary. Dr. Suess describes his fictional world as illustrations of the "out of whack." An example of the whackiness of the Suess world is a beast named Natch. For years no one has been able to see him because he's been in his cave pouting. This is a concern to the people of his community, so the enterprising young Gerald McGrew concocts a plan sure to lure the Natch from his cave.

He's going to:

Fix up a dish that is just to his taste; Three chicken cro-
quettes made of library paste, Then sprinkled with
peanut shucks, pickled and spiced, Baked at 600 degrees
and then iced.[1]

In the Suess world such a recipe succeeds in luring the
reluctant Natch back into society. In another Dr. Suess
book an elephant named Horton sits on the top of a
spindly tree, enduring the environmental rigors of chang-
ing seasons as he determines to hatch a bird egg.

There are times when we might wonder if we have
unwittingly wandered into a Dr. Suess-type world. The
events in our lives don't always coincide with our sense of
the predictable and expected. (My experience at the gas
pump is an example. Dr. Suess is quoted as saying,
"Humor has a tremendous place in a sordid world. It's
more than just a laughing matter. If you can see things
out of whack then you can see how things can be in
whack."[2] In other words, our ability to see the distinction
between what is out of whack and what is not assures us
that we have a handle on what occurrences make up a
normal world. Our perspective is clear—in balance.
Dr. Suess speaks profoundly about how we react to the
irregularities of life. A key to altering our perspective and
ensuring mental and emotional health lies in our ability
to find humor in whatever is out of joint.

Several years ago, my dear friend Luci Swindoll and I
unintentionally threw a local pastor into a zany situation.

Ken was on a business trip, and in his absence I convinced Luci to accompany me on a Sunday morning visit to a church in our area. Neither of us had ever attended the church before.

We entered the small but cozy sanctuary and were seated by a friendly usher who handed us visitor cards and whispered that they would be picked up shortly. I didn't want to fill in the requested information because I knew I would not be returning. However, not wanting to appear ungracious, I whispered to Luci that I was going to turn in the card but with a name other than my own and an out-of-state address so the visitation committee would know I was just "passing through." Luci nodded and said she would do the same.

I wrote my mother's name and the address from Vancouver, Washington where I had grown up and handed the card back to the waiting usher. Luci, before handing her card over, quickly showed me what she had written: "Miss Bernadette Apes"—with my address and phone number. I stifled a combination groan and giggle as she handed her card to the usher.

At the conclusion of the service, to my absolute horror, the pastor said, "Now, here's my favorite part of the service—the introducing of our visitors to the congregation." When he came to my card, in a stack of about fifteen, he said, "Elizabeth Ricker?" I raised my hand. "I see you're from Vancouver, Washington."

"Ah . . . yes, yes, I am."

"Well, Washington is a lovely, green state—what a beautiful place to live. I hope you'll enjoy visiting California as much as I always enjoy visiting Washington."

I nodded in weak response as he reached for the next card. He held it for just a moment in an attempt to comprehend the name.

"Uh . . . Bernadette Apes. Miss . . . Bernadette Apes? Are you here somewhere Miss Apes?"

Luci soberly raised her hand. I was biting the inside of my lip to the point of bleeding as he attempted a brief exchange with the shy, retiring Miss Apes. She assured the pastor she was a long-term resident of Fullerton and that she was a lonely person. I nearly exploded inside with laughter. I thought, *Luci—you moron—how on earth can you do the crazy things you do, especially in the name of my address and phone number?* At the conclusion of the service, we made a hasty escape to the parking lot and fell over the hood of my car in hysterics.

The following Tuesday night I was at the back of the house chatting with our daughter, Beth. Ken responded to a knock at the front door. A man whom Ken did not know said, "Could I please speak with Bernadette Apes?"

"Pardon me?" (Ken had not heard about our escapade.)

"Miss Bernadette Apes . . . may I speak with her please?"

"Well, I'm sorry, but there must be some mistake . . ."

The man held up the visitor card and asked if he was at the correct address. Ken said that the address was right, but the person was not. The man apologized and left.

After explaining the whole incident to my long-suffering husband, I was overcome with a sense of guilt and concern for the poor man who had come to our house. I was sure he had given up a relaxing evening at home to embark on a fruitless search for Miss Apes.

The next day I phoned the pastor of the church, identified myself, and confessed the whole incident. In the midst of my profuse apologizing, he emitted a beautifully rich, baritone laugh that increased in intensity until he could hardly breathe. I wanted to hug him. When he got his breath he said, "Marilyn, my wife and I went out for dinner after the service and just roared over that incident. I described to her the masterful control I exhibited in reading Miss Bernadette Apes's name and then my feelings as I attempted to talk with her. I wondered if the whole thing were on the level, but I had to keep my composure in case it were. I can't wait to tell my wife about your call."

Here is a man who saw the humor in the antics of two women during an otherwise normal Sunday morning service. He could have chosen to fret internally over the unexpected appearance of Miss Apes's name on the visitor card and then reprimand me for the incident because it threatened to make him lose his dignity and possibly disrupt the service. Instead, he chose to laugh. The following Christmas I received a card from this wonderful pastor and his wife addressed to "Miss Bernadette Apes" and signed "still smiling."

The ability to laugh over those unexpected and unwanted experiences that threaten to get the best of us enables us to change our perspective. Putting this philosophy into practice means that when something goes wrong, instead of being victimized by it, we lighten up, take the situation less seriously, and see if there isn't a laugh to be found somewhere. When we are able to do this, we are in control of our situation instead of our situation being in control of us.

Carol Burnett, in a *Los Angeles Times* interview with Charles Champlin, tells of a time when she refused to allow her situation to get the best of her. She said that as a child she had always idolized James Stewart and would, with eyes glued in rapt attention on the movie screen, watch his films over and over until she almost knew the scripts by heart. Years later, when her own career as an entertainer was flourishing, she was able to meet him. He was filming *The FBI Story* at Warner Brothers. During a break in the film, they were introduced. She says:

> He was doing a scene on a raised platform. I climbed up and we said hello, and I blurbled the usual things you say when you meet an idol, and then I stepped off the platform, putting one foot right into a bucket of whitewash that was sitting there. I never looked back. I just kept walking, dragging the bucket along with me.[3]

For those of us who enjoy the comedic brilliance of Carol Burnett, we recognize this incident as a familiar Burnett skit. But for her, at that moment, it was not a skit—it was a painful reality. Were it not for her marvelous capacity to laugh and appreciate how ludicrous she must have appeared, she might have succumbed to feelings of humiliation. Instead, it has become one of her favorite stories. James Stewart, incidentally, did not remember the incident.

To many of us, the experience of tripping and falling in front of a large group of people would be so devastating we would be unable to do anything but slink under the stairs and refuse to emerge. But to react in that way would allow our circumstances to control us. That would be leaving our perceptions out of whack.

The examples I have used to illustrate the value of humor as an aid to regaining control of our circumstances have been lighthearted. I do not mean to imply that humor is limited to our lighter experiences only. I believe that even in our pain, in the deepest anguish of our souls, the ability to be less intense and to enjoy some humor can give relief and help bring restoration. That moment of humor may be offset by days or weeks of sadness, but I maintain that even one moment can do more to restore our balance than we can imagine. Let me cite a very personal example.

For two years I watched the body of my mother slowly, relentlessly, painfully gnarl up on her left side. The gnarling began with her fingers and progressed to her wrist, her arm, her shoulder, and finally her left leg, so that she could no longer walk. The pain was excruciating. Doctors were perplexed; conscientious, but ineffectual. The overwhelming debilitation rendered her almost helpless. The constant pain changed her personality as she could barely think beyond what she felt. Believe me, I did more crying than laughing during those two years.

I absolutely adored my mother. I am an only child—my mother has been wonderful to me all my life. It grieved me beyond description to see her in this state. In November of 1983, in a desperate attempt to alleviate the pain, Mom elected to have a very delicate brain surgery designed to sear off those nerve endings that were sending pain signals throughout her left side. The risk was great but the pain was greater. She survived the surgery but was plagued with repeated bouts of pneumonia afterward. On January 7, 1984, she died. I was devastated. I still am. Of course I am so glad she's in a painless eternity with the Jesus she loved and served. But I miss her—I always will.

Mom had asked that her body be cremated. She always felt there was something pagan about the dressing and funeral reverencing of a body whose function is merely to house an immortal soul. On the day I picked up the little box that contained my mother's ashes, I experienced a peculiar sensation as I tried to grasp the reality I was experiencing. I would never again see what was visually familiar to me about my mother. What I was carrying in my hands was completely foreign.

Ken was waiting in the front seat of the car. As I opened the door with the box in my hands, his eyes were averted in an attempt to be more casual about that moment than either of us felt. As I placed the box on the seat, there was an awkward moment of silence. I broke that silence with a quiet, "Mom, would you like a seat belt?" Ken looked startled and I laughed—not hard and loud—but it felt good. My mom would have understood—in fact, she would have joined me. For a few minutes, my hurt was diminished—less intense. It was a painful moment relieved by a quiet laugh. It restored my control.

You may feel there are times in life that simply will not yield even an ounce of humor. May I suggest that during those seemingly interminable times of pain, you fight to see beyond the restrictive confines of the immediate; remind yourself that those moments will not last forever. Whatever it is that threatens to crush your spirit and claim your joy today will not necessarily be there tomorrow, next month, or next year. Life moves forward and circumstances change. You will not always be in a pit! That reminder in itself brings a respite to the soul. From there perhaps a glimmer of light can seep through the darkness, enabling you to search out that seemingly elusive but spirit-lifting smile or laugh that helps you regain control.

In spite of this chapter's emphasis upon personal control, I am not suggesting that we are ever totally in control of our circumstances. Ephesians 1:11 reminds us that God, in his sovereign love and power "works all things after the counsel of His will." My security, my rest, my peace, and my joy live always in the sure knowledge of that comforting truth. But God invites my participation in the executing of his divine will for my life. To me, a part of that participation has to do with how I perceive the events of my life. I determine whether or not I'm going to view my experiences through a negative or a positive lens. If indeed my perceptions are negative, then it stands to reason my life will feel out of whack, and like the Natch, I can spend years pouting in my cave. Thank God I don't have to pout, fuss, or complain; I have the option to smile, chuckle, or laugh. When I do, in that arena where God invites my participation, I am in control.

We Are Restored

3

*H*enry Ward Beecher stated that "A person without a sense of humor is like a wagon without springs—jolted by every pebble in the road." Humor can work as a safety valve to relieve stress that might otherwise continue to build and damage our health.

Several years ago I was giving a final exam to one of my American Literature classes when a student, obviously feeling stressed, raised his hand to ask permission to tell a joke. I sensed the class would benefit from a break, so I told him to feel free. This was his joke:

Lawyer: "I can't believe that at age eighty-seven, after sixty-eight years of marriage, you would want a divorce."

Old Man: "The marriage never worked. I never loved

her . . . certainly didn't like her . . . I want out . . . just get me a divorce."

Lawyer: "But if you've been so miserable for all these years, why did you wait until now to try for a divorce?"

Old Man: "We made an agreement that we would stay together until the children died."

There was a slight pause from the class as they internalized that unexpected punch line; then they erupted into spontaneous laughter. They laughed because they were reacting to stress and sought to alleviate it. Interestingly enough, after a few minutes the classroom became extremely quiet as each student returned with renewed commitment to the lamentable task at hand. That moment of laughter, a number of students told me later, proved to be a great attitude changer and a boost to performance. (I don't remember if their test scores gave like testimony.)

Dr. Hans Selye, an authority on stress, claims that stress is the nonspecific response of the body to any demand made upon it. It is immaterial whether the situation we face is pleasant or unpleasant. All that counts is the intensity of the demand for readjustment. Any arousal state produces a physiological imbalance that demands restoration. Since the body's store of adaptive energy required to restore this balance is limited, the body is not capable of accommodating unlimited stress.

Humankind's inability to withstand unlimited stress

is becoming a source of increasing concern in corporate America. More and more organizations are hiring firms to provide programs to motivate employees to reduce their level of stress. Laugh therapist Bob Basso, whom I heard at a stress-reduction conference, stated that 52 percent of us would die from stress or stress-related illnesses in the next thirty years. His remedy: Have fun when you can and laugh even when you can't. The alternative is to experience an inevitable eroding of health.

When we examine the body's physiological responses to laughter, we can see why it is an effective stress reliever. Laboratory experiments reveal that laughter is accompanied by a decrease in tone of the skeletal muscles of the body. We have all experienced that feeling of becoming weak all over, perhaps even collapsing, when we are seized by a fit of hearty laughter. We suddenly go limp. Theorists have pointed out that laughter involves a release of tension or a release of surplus energy, which, in turn, causes our muscles to relax.

Laughter is also prescribed for the seriously ill. A wonderful organization in Southern California, Carousel of Clowns, is quick to testify to the therapeutic benefits of laughter. For years caravans of these caring volunteer clowns have brought cheer to patients in hospitals and care facilities, providing entertainment for the mentally and physically handicapped. Their shows are designed to achieve maximum audience participation and reaction with fast-paced music, dance, and mime, and enough suspense to hold the limited attention spans of mentally ill patients. A sing-along ends their show with all the clowns on stage and most of their audience joining in. At Harbor View House in San Pedro, a nonprofit mental-health center for about two hundred mentally ill patients, I witnessed an incredible change in spirit as the residents responded to the fun these clowns brought to their mirthless lives.

Dr. Raymond Moody in his book *Laugh After Laugh: The Healing Power of Humor* makes some interesting observations about the role of clowns in bringing people back from severely withdrawn and unresponsive states, even after all attempts by their doctors and nurses have failed. He related an incident of a well-known clown whose face, because of television, would be familiar to most American children. While visiting in a large hospital, the clown saw a little girl with a doll that looked like him lying beside her as she was being fed by a nurse. As the clown walked into her room, the child said his name. The nurse threw down the spoon and ran off to call the doctor. The child had been diagnosed as catatonic and had been unresponsive for six months. The doctor was able to get her to follow up this first communication with other responses. The child progressively improved following this breakthrough.

Dr. Moody relates another case of a ninety-five-year-old man who was admitted to the hospital with severe depression. He had not eaten or spoken for several days. His doctors were concerned that he would soon die. A clown entered his hospital room and within thirty minutes had succeeded in getting the elderly man to talk, to laugh, and to eat. The man lived for several more years and the clown maintained communication with him during that time.

There are a number of reports in medical literature of persons who have been cured of physical illness, or at least greatly helped, by the use of laughter and humor. One of the best known cases of laughter helping to combat serious illness is that of Norman Cousins, author and former longtime editor of the *Saturday Review* magazine. In his best-selling book *Anatomy of an Illness*, Cousins details his remarkable recovery from a potentially fatal illness. Following a stress-filled trip abroad, he suffered from a serious collagen disease, a disorder of the connective tissue. The doctor explained there was no cure for the disease and that it would get progressively worse until the patient became physically rigid.

Cousins began his own private battle against the illness. After thorough research, he designed, with the cooperation of his doctor, his own plan for recovery. He gave up painkillers and began large intravenous doses of vitamin C. Reasoning that positive emotions have positive effects on the body, he began to fight the pain with laughter. He obtained some funny movies—specifically, some old *Candid Camera* segments as well as many Marx

Brothers films. He discovered that one ten-minute interlude of laughter produced two hours of painless sleep. He also noted that each session of laughter caused a reduction of inflammation and that the effect was cumulative. His self-administered program also included a nutritious diet. He continued to improve, and more than a decade later when he wrote his account, he was enjoying a complete restoration of health.

Norman Cousins calls laughter a form of internal jogging. He says that in responding to the initial phase of a typical joke, comedy routine, or story, muscle tension increases in anticipation of the climax of the story or punch line. Immediately following the story climax, the chest, abdomen, and face get a vigorous workout. In convulsive laughter even the legs and arms are involved. During this phase, heart rate, breathing, and circulation speed up. When the spasm of laughter subsides, the pulse rate drops below normal and the muscles relax. During the laughter response the body is revitalized by what is sometimes called internal massage.

It is hard to believe that laughter caused a reduction in the inflammation of Cousins's joints, and yet, that fact is medically documented. Interesting research is now being done that suggests humor may directly attack the pain associated with inflammatory conditions such as arthritis, gout, and those resulting from certain injuries. This research gives added credence to Cousins's experience.

According to Dr. Moody, laughter stimulates the brain to produce the alertness hormone, catecholamine—a complex substance that contains epinephrine, norepinephrine, and dopamine and enables us to respond physically to emergencies. In turn, the arousal hormone stimulates the release of endorphins—the body's natural painkillers. As the brain's level of endorphins increases, the perception of pain decreases. Laughter, then, causes the body to produce its own painkiller.

I love to see the truth of Scripture confirmed by secular sciences. God has prescribed a joyful heart as good medicine and scientists are now saying our body's natural painkillers are released when we laugh. The oft-repeated scriptural imperative "rejoice" takes on new significance as we realize what happens physiologically when we do rejoice. God means for us to experience joy. It is not his intent that we suffer from ulcers, migraine headaches, and other stress-related illnesses. Review with me these scriptures that remind us what God says about joy.

"A cheerful heart has a continual feast" (Proverbs 15:15).

"A joyful heart makes a cheerful face" (Proverbs 15:13).

"They will find gladness and joy, and sorrow and sighing will flee away" (Isaiah 35:10).

"For I will turn their mourning into joy, and will comfort them, and give them joy for their sorrow" (Jeremiah 31:13).

"And let Thy godly ones sing for joy" (Psalm 132:9).

"Why are you in despair, O my soul? And why are you disturbed within me? Hope in God, for I shall again praise Him, the help of my countenance and my God" (Psalm 43:5).

Our hope is indeed in God, the source of our joy. If we are not experiencing joy, perhaps David's prayer in Psalm 51:12 could be ours: "Restore to me the joy of Thy salvation, and sustain me with a willing spirit." Our salvation is Jesus; because of him, we anticipate an everlasting eternity with the God of the universe. Before that eternity is ours, however, we live out our days on this earth. We want to live them with joy. We want to live them with health.

God has given to each of us an incomparable medicine bag—in it is the divinely created ability to laugh at ourselves, at our circumstances, at humor produced by others, and to take a less threatened view of everything around us. To utilize the contents of that bag is to experience healing for our minds, our souls, and our bodies.

We Are Witnesses

4

I would like to make a distinction between the experience of joy and the act of laughing. I believe Scripture teaches that there is a wellspring of joy within each believing heart and God means to suffuse our innermost beings with it. Many people know that joy but do not necessarily express it in overt laughter. A nonlaughing person is not necessarily a nonjoyful person. However, I view laughter as an intensifier of my joy. When I experience laughter as well as joy, I double my pleasure! But for the purposes of this chapter I would like to focus on the believer's joy and its benefits, not on the actual pursuit of humor or laughter. In doing so, let me begin by flashing back to an especially moving graduation exercise at Biola University.

Certain moments in life guarantee a lump in my throat and a tear in my eye. One such moment is hearing "Pomp and Circumstance" and watching eager graduates in cap and gown parade down the aisle—each step taking them farther from that matriculation into a new phase of life. In spite of the many Biola graduations in which I have participated, that momentous occasion never fails to move me.

At Biola graduations each young man or woman is introduced by name and walks across the platform to receive the congratulatory handshake from the president. For one brief moment, the graduate has the stage and, as classmates, faculty, and proud, sacrificing parents look on, his or her hard work is recognized apart from that of the entire class. During this portion of the ceremony at one particular graduation, a student named Dave made his uncertain way to the platform. When his name was announced, he crossed the stage with noticeable deliberation. As he shook hands with the president, his classmates leaped to their feet in an exuberant ovation which continued for several minutes. Why the ovation? Dave was blind; we had all watched him cheerfully navigate the sprawling campus for four years, refusing to yield to his handicap. His infectious laugh, his warmth, and his indomitable spirit were an inspiration to the sometimes flagging spirits of his sighted classmates. So when we saw Dave in his moment of commemoration, it was impossible not to cheer, or feel a lump in the throat, or wipe away a tear.

I remember one afternoon my office door was open, and Dave wandered in stopping just short of my desk. Since he had managed to escape me for the nine units of required English, we were not personally acquainted. Before I could speak, he laughed quietly and said, "I have a sense that I'm not in Dr. Sturz's office." I told him that Dr. Sturz's office was next door—he had come one office too far. Again he laughed and said, "I knew I was in a woman's office because it smells so good; men never smell that good." I disagreed with him and said I'd follow the scent of Grey Flannel aftershave anywhere. That exchange precipitated a most engaging conversation of nearly thirty minutes. During that time I noted his frequent, nonself-conscious laugh as we exchanged remarks. Finally, I commented on his lightheartedness and asked him to tell me how he could adopt such a cheerful stance. I'll never forget his response. He began a paraphrase of portions of Psalm 139.

God has searched me and known me. He knows when I sit down and when I rise up. He understands my thoughts from afar. He scrutinizes my path and my lying down and is intimately acquainted with all my ways. God has enclosed me behind and before, and laid His hand upon me. His hand will lead me.

As Dave rose to leave he said, "So you see, Mrs. Meberg, if God always sees where I am even if I don't, I figure I'm on the right path. That thought always makes me happy."

Dave's optimism did not originate in a humanistic philosophy that espouses positive thinking in spite of it all. His cheer sprang from a far deeper source—the sure conviction that God had his best interests at heart and had promised to keep his hand upon Dave.

What greater testimony can we give an unbelieving world than a cheerful, joyful demeanor that bespeaks an unshakable faith in the provision of an almighty God? That attitude says far more to others than any number of words and phrases we might offer in the vain hope that we are being a positive witness. The truth of the cliché, "Your actions speak so loudly I can't hear what you say," is sobering as we consider the attitudes we can reflect to those around us.

Cheerfulness and joy are not moral requirements for Christian living, but I do believe they are a consequence, an inevitable result, of our faith in God. When we attempt to generate joy within ourselves apart from God, it is sporadic at best. Ultimately, we sense the inability and depletedness of our own humanity.

Eugene H. Peterson in his book *A Long Obedience in the Same Direction* says:

We cannot make ourselves joyful. Joy cannot be commanded, purchased, or arranged. But there is something we can do. We can decide to live in response to the abundance of God, and not under the dictatorship of our own poor needs. We can decide to live in the environment of a living God and not our own dying selves. [1]

Our joy, our ability to laugh in the face of difficulties, has more to do with how we view God than how he views us. At times many of us fear that maybe God isn't all that interested in our daily lives. We've been taught the His-eye-is-on-the-sparrow-so-we-know-he-watches-us mentality, but we are far from convinced. Sometimes we see our lives running counter to our desires, wishes, and prayers; we then assume God doesn't care. When these kinds of thoughts take over and undermine our faith, we have ceased to live in "response to the abundance of God."

The key word in this phrase is *response*. Most of us have a good head-knowledge of God's abundance, but we often find ourselves unable to respond to that abundance. That inability to respond possibly comes from a growing fear that God is truly unaware of where we are and how we are. When this happens, we need bolstering, and there's no better source for faith-bolstering than God's living Word.

There are several verses in the twenty-ninth chapter of Jeremiah that invariably renew my vigor as well as my faith whenever I lose my vision of the abundance of God:

"For I know the plans that I have for you," declares the LORD, "plans for welfare and not for calamity to give you a future and a hope. Then you will call upon Me and come and pray to me, and I will listen to you. And you will seek Me and find Me, when you search for Me with all your heart" (vv. 11–13).

When I am reminded that God has a plan for me that is for my welfare and that promises a future as well as a hope, I feel like David when he said, "By my God, I can leap over a wall" (Psalm 18:29). I am not on a haphazard course of my own poor choosing. Psalm 16:11 assures me "Thou wilt make known to me the path of life." I choose to believe God will indeed make life's path known to me, and that where I am on that path is no surprise to him.

In order for us to feel the assurance that God has an individual plan for us, we need to be convinced that he is aware of us as individuals in the first place. I love the passage in Matthew 10:30 that says, "But the very hairs of your head are all numbered." Isn't that mind-boggling personal awareness? In case we're tempted to think that verse just so much biblical rhetoric, let's review the life of a woman in Scripture who illustrates God's individual care and concern.

Do you remember Rahab's story in the second chapter of Joshua? She was living in Jericho, a city whose collective acts of idolatry, sexual perversion, and moral corruption were known around the country. Jericho was the first city to be conquered by the Israelites as they laid claim to the promised land God had promised to Abraham centuries earlier. The Israelites were understandably eager to "get on with it," but God was aware of the budding faith of a woman in Jericho named Rahab. God directed Joshua to send some spies into Jericho. Once in the city, the spies amazingly enough found themselves in Rahab's house, about whom they knew nothing. (This fact is not amazing at all when one considers God's style!) This is the one house in the city whose occupant would not only welcome them but also hide them from the spies of her own king. While they were in her home, Rahab gave witness to her belief in the Israelite God by saying "for the LORD your God, He is God in heaven above and on earth beneath (Joshua 2:11)." At her request for safety, the Israelites made a pact with her that if she would hang a long scarlet cord down the side of the wall (her house was on the wall), they promised to protect her from any destruction that would come to the city and its inhabitants.

When the city of Jericho was subsequently surrounded by the Israelites and the walls came crashing down, there remained one portion of wall down which trailed a scarlet cord. There waited a woman for whom God had momentarily halted the progress of over two million people in order to make provision for the welfare of one.

Living in response to the abundance of God is simply having the faith to rest in his provision and to believe in his individual caring. The familiar Philippians 4:19 passage states, "My God shall supply all your needs according to

His riches in glory in Christ Jesus." These are joy-producing scriptural reminders. They can strengthen our faith because when our faith is strengthened, our joy returns. When our joy returns, so does our smile. That smile then becomes a positive witness to the reality of our faith.

Our faith is enlivened as we contemplate God's provision and sovereign control over the world. I love 2 Chronicles 20:6, "O LORD, the God of our fathers, art Thou not God in the heavens? And art Thou not ruler over all the kingdoms and the nations? Power and might are in Thy hand so that no one can stand against Thee." Doesn't that verse buoy your spirits? God's in control! He rules all the kingdoms and all the nations; nobody stands against him! Jesus reminded us of that when he said, "In the world you have tribulation, but take courage; I have overcome the world" (John 16:33). The reason believers in Christ can have a cheerful demeanor, can have joy, and can laugh heartily is because we're on the side that has overcome. In the face of life's tribulations Jesus exhorts us to take courage because he has overcome the world.

Scripture tells us that Jesus' death and resurrection overcame death as well. Isaiah 25:8 says, "He will swallow up death for all time, and the Lord GOD will wipe tears away from all faces." What a fantastic truth—the swallowing up of death—the removal of tears! "O Death, where is your victory? O Death, where is your sting?" (1 Corinthians 15:55). There is no sting! Jesus eliminated it. That sounds so good to me it makes me smile. In fact, I could laugh for joy.

Laughing for joy in relation to death has taken on a new significance for me since my mother passed away. Eleven or twelve hours following her death I was in the shower, which often serves as my sanctuary, and was thinking about my mom. I tried to internalize the enormity of what had happened that day. She was at that very moment in heaven. What did she feel? What was it like? She was actually in the presence of God! I tried to visualize her in her new surroundings; as I did, I became lost to my own. A vision of my mother began to appear on the screen of my mind. I saw her in the arms of Jesus. He was holding her as one would a child, cradling her against his body. Her face was radiant and as Jesus held her, he began to gently swing her back and forth in his arms. Back and forth—back and forth—and she began to laugh and laugh, until her head was thrown back in total abandonment. At first I was a bit startled by this image of my mother, but as joy and relief flooded over me I thought, *Well, of course. She can laugh now. She hasn't laughed in two years; not even smiled in six months. But God has wiped away all her tears and now she can laugh again . . . and again . . . and again.* "There is an appointed time for everything . . . a time to weep and a time to laugh" (Ecclesiastes 3:1,4). It was my mother's time to laugh.

Now, I am not prone to visions; I don't believe I've ever had one before. I'm not even sure what I think about people who claim to have them. Perhaps psychology would say that I had unwittingly placed upon my mother's image a wish-projection. Whatever the explanation (and there is much to life that defies explanation), the image of my mother's carefree laughing not only comforted me, but inspired a concept that I love. And that is, we as believers in Christ, who conquered death, have the last laugh. As we walk through this life, we encounter pain, we encounter heartache, and we encounter sorrow. But at the end of it all, we encounter God! The last laugh is ours!

Why We
part
2
Don't Laugh

"A broken spirit dries up the bones."

We Aren't Valued

5

One of the most debilitating spirit-breakers I know is the tendency to judge the worth of others as well as ourselves on the basis of performance. With this mind-set we assume that if what is done is good, so is the person. If what is done is not good, neither is the person.

When I was in the seventh grade, I had an experience in my sewing class which, if my person were evaluated on the basis of my performance, I would score a zero! I had come into the class optimistically expecting to master the art of sewing within the first few weeks. My confidence was reinforced by the teacher's promise that we could all become expert seamstresses by the end of the semester.

The first week of class was entitled "Knowing Our Machine." I soon discovered my machine had no desire to be known. In fact, it had no interest in a relationship whatsoever! I watched intently as our teacher demonstrated the intricate maze the thread had to follow from the spool to the needle. Every time I thought I had successfully completed each step and pressed the lever to begin the magical process of sewing, the thread would be slurped up by some unknown force and flail wildly about on the spool. Threading the machine was not the only difficulty I experienced.

To the left of the needle there is a little trap door where the bobbin lives. On the third day of class, for some inexplicable reason, my bobbin chose to fling itself out upon the floor and go racing across the room. The thread was bright red and left a telltale path to my machine. At this point my classmates gleefully assumed my ineptitude would provide them innumerable laughs throughout the semester. The teacher, however, did not appear to relish that prospect. As she loomed over my machine with errant bobbin in hand, she said in carefully controlled tones, "Apparently we don't know our machine."

The second week of class was entitled "Knowing Our Patterns." Since my relationship with my machine was definitely not a friendly one, I approached my patterns with a bit of anxiety. In no time, patterns proved to be as great a mystery as machines. The paper was so thin and crinkly that the anxiety-induced perspiration on my hands caused the paper to stick to my palms so that I continually had to peel it off and use my elbow to position the pattern on the cloth. With this basic step finally accomplished, I was supposed to cut the cloth from around the pattern. I assumed that side A and side B were properly pinned and, when cut, would produce one piece; that's how it worked for everyone else. But somehow, when I unfolded the material, instead of a whole piece of fabric, I had side A in my left hand and side B in my right hand.

The project for the class was to make a pair of pajamas. I chose a flannel fabric with little pink rosebuds. Perhaps you are aware that repeated ripping and sewing causes the threads in the fabric to separate and the design to become indistinguishable. It soon became impossible to discern if there were rosebuds, windmills, or frogs in the design.

As the semester progressed and I did not, I was in serious danger of failing. I was horrified—I had never failed a class before. I needed much more help than I felt free to ask for, because by now the teacher had adopted a certain stance toward me which was very disconcerting. She had the most peculiar response any time she saw me heading toward her desk with my fragile pajamas extended before me. She would begin to take in air, and the longer I remained at her desk the more she inhaled. There were times when I was sure she doubled in size, nearly filling her end of the room. Not only was I inhibited by this response, I was also unable to distinguish what she said as the sucked-in air whistled slightly through her clenched teeth. I would usually flee from her desk in defeat and relief as the audible expulsion of breath signaled that she had once again survived her massive inhalations.

The day before the class was over everyone else had completed their project, but I was still working fervidly in an attempt to finish my pajamas. Shortly before the bell rang, I triumphantly put in the final stitch. I gingerly took the pajamas up to the teacher for her final inspection. To my dismay, through clenched teeth she ordered me to "Try them on." I did not think the fabric could withstand the pressure of my body. She was adamant, however, so I complied. I could not believe my eyes. I had sewn the left leg into the right arm and the right arm into the left leg. I tried every possible way to scrunch up my body so that maybe I could get by with them as they were, but one would have to have been far more deformed than I to pass them off as a good fit.

My friend Jane, when she recovered from hysterics, promised to help me take out each wrong stitch with a straight pin after school and then pin the leg and the arm into their proper places. All I would have to do the next day was put in the final stitches. It seemed simple enough. The next day I settled down with my machine and began to sew very carefully. Within twenty minutes I had finished. I leaped jubilantly to my feet with the intention of rushing up to my teacher to show her my now completed project. In my haste, I neglected to pull the lever up to release the needle from the cloth. My sudden movement of jumping up without first releasing the pajamas knocked the machine off balance. As I stepped back from the falling machine, I realized I had inadvertently sewn my skirt into the pajama top so that I could not free myself from the material or the fall. I flew over the top of the machine as if I were on the end of a whip. I sprawled on the floor in final surrender to that piece of equipment which had sought to defeat me all semester. My wonderful friends shrieked in hysterics; for once, the teacher did not begin her usual inhalations; she merely put her head down on her desk. Finally Jane cut me loose with giant pinking shears. I borrowed a skirt from the dressing room; Jane got my skirt out of the pajamas, sewed the leg and arm in properly, and the dismally frayed pajamas were turned in later that day.

This story always succeeds in getting a good laugh, especially when I tell it at mother/daughter banquets featuring style shows of home-sewn clothes. But in the seventh grade when I was experiencing repeated failure, I found little cause for humor. My teacher was looking for good performance. She fawned over Mary Beth, who seemed to have been born with a thimble in her hand. Everything Mary Beth made looked as if it could have been bought off the rack at Sak's Fifth Avenue. But whenever I approached the teacher's desk, the smile would fade, her eyebrows would draw together, and she would begin her unnerving inhalations. Somehow my triumph of the moment, whether it was sewing a seam that only wobbled in one small place or finally setting in a sleeve after the fifth try, dwindled to nothing under her disapproving scrutiny. Something inside me would begin to whisper, "It's not good enough, Marilyn. You're not as good a seamstress as Mary Beth; you're not even as good a person as Mary Beth!" My teacher's thinly disguised disdain for me and my performance caused me to feel devalued as a person.

Though I failed miserably as a seamstress, I did not fail as a person. Fortunately, I was raised by parents who made me feel valued apart from what I did. When I performed well, naturally they were pleased. But when I did not do something well, I did not lose their love or support. My sense of personal worth was regained from their acceptance of me despite my sewing incompetence and D grade. My broken spirit was healed.

In fact, not only was my broken spirit healed, I soon began to laugh about my experience. My dad told me some weeks after the class was over that though he and Mom felt sorry for me as I muddled my way through sewing, they also had to exercise tremendous self-control as I would daily apprise them of my hard-to-believe errors. On several occasions they laughed uncontrollably when they were alone. Mom told me that she had never been able to grasp the details of sewing, absolutely abhorred the class she had to take in high school, and hoped never to see a sewing machine again. We began to laugh about the incidences from our respective classes until finally, one of our standing family jokes was to include a request for a sewing machine on our Christmas list each year. One of my Dad's favorite lines, even now, is to admire something I'm wearing and then with mock seriousness ask if I made it myself.

Because I had a foundation of acceptance and support, my spirit was healed and I was released to see the humor; I could laugh. Without that acceptance, not only would I not be inclined to laugh, I would be reduced to living with the assumption that my value, my personal worth, was predicated upon my performance.

I have had scores of students who could not separate their academic performance from their worth as persons. As long as their grades were high, they felt good about themselves. If their grades slipped, so did their sense of worth. It is a common error to assume we are worthy persons as long as we perform well. With that mind-set, we believe that what we do is more valuable than who we are.

When we make such an assumption, we reduce ourselves and others to objects or things. Objects are expected to perform well; when they don't, they are replaced. If, for instance, my car repeatedly breaks down on the freeway, I am going to become so exasperated with its poor performance that I'll try to get rid of it and buy a new one. If my dishwasher persists, even after repeated repairs, to spew water all over the kitchen walls, I will either stop using it or replace it. We have a right to expect a good performance from objects whose only purpose is to perform a function. Unfortunately, we often use the same logic when it comes to ourselves and others.

Admittedly, communication with bank tellers, receptionists, registration clerks, etc., is usually impersonal and objective. For instance, when I go through the checkout line in a new grocery store I respond as an object and I am treated as an object.

"Will there be anything else?"

"No, thank you."

"That will be $423.62."

"Do you take Master Card?"

"No."

"Library card?"

But communication with family members and others we love or work with ought not to be. Treating those we love like objects can be so subtly done we may not even be aware we are doing it.

When our children were growing up, the before-bed routine was to have a little devotional time with each of them individually. We often had a Bible verse for the week which was memorized and quoted; we talked about what it meant and how it could be applied to our lives, and then we prayed together. Beth, who had a particular facility for memorization, learned a new hymn each week in addition to a verse. She was only four years old when we began this program of memorizing and singing. I was delighted with our exemplary time of devotions each evening.

One night as I was leaving Beth's room, I was overcome with self-congratulatory praise. Beth had just flawlessly sung all three verses of "What a Friend We Have in Jesus," quoted her verse for the week, and prayed about everything from the wobbly front wheel of her tricycle to the hope that we might have pancakes for breakfast in the morning. *You're doing a great job, Marilyn. I wish Ken were home tonight to have heard Beth, to see how responsive she is to our training. With the rich environment she is privileged to live in, she'll become another Mother Teresa, giving tirelessly of herself to others when she grows up.*

These egotistical musings were abruptly interrupted as Beth called me back into her room. I gazed fondly down on our budding little saint as she leaned up on one elbow and announced to me, "You know, Mommy, I don't believe any of that stuff we do every night." I stared at her in astonishment. "What do you mean? What don't you believe?" She was very quiet for a few minutes and then firmly said, "I think you made it all up." And then as if to comfort me she added, "But that's all right, Mommy, don't feel bad—it's nice stuff." I could not believe my ears. All those nights of careful indoctrination and she thought I simply made it up. I felt like saying, "How can you possibly know what you're talking about? You're only four years old. Believe it! Believe it because it's true. It's true because I say it's true."

In my mind, at that moment, I had reduced Beth to an object. What she thought and then said did not please me.

I had been pleased with her earlier performances of singing hymns and quoting Scripture. I wanted her to do and be as I desired. But Beth is not an object. She is a human being who dared to be honest and question the truth of what she was being taught.

We are concerned about how our children perform because they reflect either positively or negatively upon our performance as parents. We would like to convince ourselves that we can expect certain things of them because we know what is best for them. In many instances we do know what is best, but in many others what we want to pass off as being for them is for us. We want to look good as well as feel good about ourselves. Much of my devastation with Beth's rejection of what I was teaching her was that her rejection called my performance into question. I was failing somehow as a mother. What was I doing wrong? How could I change her so I would feel better about myself as a parent? Those kinds of questions reflect an unhealthy self-absorption whose main concern is not for the child but for the image of the parent.

At work we may spend years with our fellow employees, seeing in them only their successes or failures and knowing nothing of their inner life because they are merely objects to us. When they succeed and that success enhances our work environment, we are pleased they have functioned well. When they fail, and that failure inconveniences us, we are irritated. Paul Tournier in his excellent book *The Meaning of Persons* claims that when we cease to see people as objects and begin to see them as persons, all one's professional relationships take on a new character.

> They become shot through with a joy that was absent when they were merely the fulfilling of a function. Everything becomes an occasion for personal contact, a chance to understand others and the personal factors which underlie their behavior, their reactions and opinions. It is much more interesting, as well as important, to understand why someone has a certain failing, than to be irritated by it; to understand why he maintains a certain point of view than to combat it; to listen to confidences rather than to judge by appearances. [1]

There have been many times when someone ceased to be an object of irritation to me once I heard his or her heart, listened to his or her insecurities, and watched the protective mask slowly lower as I revealed my own insecurities. When I heard that heart beat in such close synchronization with my own, the person ceased to be an object. That would never have occurred without time and concentration upon our respective persons. Such a focus caused me to understand as well as empathize with what had formerly irritated me. As a result, the person ceased being a performing object and became a valuable person.

The greatest example of seeing the worth of the person apart from performance was set by Jesus. He consistently cut through the externals of performance to the interior of the heart, and each time he affirmed the worth of that individual by the way he treated him. In John 4 we read about the Samaritan woman whom Jesus met at the well. She was dumbfounded that he should even speak to her much less show an interest in who she was. Two things amazed the woman: that Jesus would ask something of her when custom dictated that a rabbi avoid contact with women in public, and that he would speak to a Samaritan. The Jews despised Samaritans because they had intermarried and mongrelized the race. Jesus ignored custom and cultural prejudice. He looked past this woman's immoral lifestyle and into her heart. Seeing her emotional and spiritual need, he offered her living water that would eternally quench her spirit's thirst. Her performance did not stop Jesus from waiting for her at the well. He recognized her need and sought to alleviate that need by becoming her Savior.

In the eighth chapter of John we read about another immoral woman, this one caught in adultery. The scribes and the Pharisees gleefully dragged her into the temple where Jesus was teaching—hoping to trap him into supporting their law that she should be stoned for her offense. Jesus turned the tables on them and said, "He who is without sin among you, let him be the first to throw a stone at her." One by one they all disappeared until Jesus was left alone with the woman. Once again he looked past her performance to the needy heart within and told her to go and "sin no more" (v. 11).

We made reference to Rahab in chapter 4 as an illustration of God's awareness of us as individuals. She also illustrates God's concern with the human heart as opposed to human performance. Her prostitution did not prevent God from making specific provision for her. He saw in Rahab the desire to be cleansed and to become a follower as well as a worshiper of Jehovah God. Who she was and who she could become were of greater importance to God than who she had been and what she had done.

Jesus says in John 13:34 that we are to "love one another, even as I have loved you." Just as Jesus first considered the worth of the person, so must we. Though someone's performance may displease us, our role is not to judge, alienate, or condemn. The cleansing of sin and the modification of behavior is God's job. The recognition of the inestimable worth of each of God's children is ours.

As we consider our role in loving one another rather then judging one another, we need to remember there is a vast difference between acceptance and approval. We are not mandated to approve of wrong behavior. Jesus did not approve of the adulterous behavior of the woman at the well, but he did accept her as one worthy of his love and provision. There is also a distinction to be made between compassion and permissiveness. To feel compassion for the misdeeds of others need not imply that a spirit of permissiveness is eroding our standards. It simply means that we recognize the worth of others and our behavior reflects a caring, warm receptivity to them in spite of what they've done.

It is easy to nod our heads in agreement that we must indeed follow the example of Christ as we love and accept each other. But it is not so easy to translate that truth into the very core of our being so that our responses to each other spring from that core.

Two years ago, Ken and I witnessed the struggle of some friends of ours as they reeled with the news that their nineteen-year-old daughter would have to drop out of college because she was pregnant. She was a straight-A student with aspirations for medical school. The baby's father, whom she loved almost desperately, was also a straight-A student with aspirations for medical school. Though he took financial responsibility for the resultant medical expenses, he would not marry the girl because he was not sure he loved her and he wanted nothing to interfere with his plan to become a doctor. The girl's parents were devastated. Theirs was a sincere and solid Christian home. Their daughter had been a prominent and enthusiastic leader in the youth activities of the church since she was in junior high school. "How could such an experience descend so unexpectedly upon us?" they asked. There was no warning—suddenly their dreams for their daughter were shattered with one tearful conversation on an otherwise uneventful Saturday afternoon. Abortion was not an option since both daughter and parents felt such an action unthinkable.

As the months progressed, we watched the parents draw the cords of love ever more securely around their "fallen" daughter. The humiliation and disappointment were at times overwhelming, but never once was that daughter made to feel alienated from the love of her parents. The baby was born and the agonizing decision not to give her up for adoption stirred much unsolicited comment from observers who had, from the beginning, felt the situation warranted disciplining as well as advice.

Last fall the young mother enrolled once again in school. The fun-filled sounds of dormitory living will never reach her ears. The dream of medical school has been replaced with the more quickly attainable teaching credential. The consequence of one night of unrestrained loving will ever be with her. But in spite of these sobering realizations, this young woman has experienced the incomparable love of Jesus reflected through the tenderness and unfailing support of her parents.

He does not treat us as our sins deserve or repay us according to our iniquities. For as high as the heavens are above the earth, so great is his love for those who fear him; as far as the east is from the west, so far has he removed our transgressions from us. As a father has compassion on his children, so the LORD has compassion on those who fear him. (Psalm 103:10–13, NIV)

God never views us as objects. He views us as valued, honored, deeply loved members of his creation. We don't have to perform for him—we serve him, and when we serve him out of love and gratitude, there is no sense of duty, obligation, or performance. Being the recipients of such unconditional love and regard can release us to experiece the joy of loving God in return. That joyful loving produces healing for our souls. That healing gives birth to the laugh impulse.

The last time I saw the young woman with the baby born out of wedlock, she and her mother were in one of our shopping malls. Grandma was pushing the stroller, baby was asleep and daughter and mother were licking Häagen-Dazs ice cream cones. It was wonderful to see them both laughing. Their pain would perhaps never be forgotten, but the inclination to laugh was restored because their sense of personal worth is assured.

> For I am convinced that neither death, nor life, nor angels, nor principalities, nor things present, nor things to come, nor powers, nor height, nor depth, nor any other created thing, shall be able to separate us from the love of God, which is in Christ Jesus our Lord. (Romans 8:38–39)

We Aren't Heard

6

A young graduate student at a major university placed an ad in a local newspaper stating he would listen to anyone, uninterruptedly, for thirty minutes if the person would simply call the number listed in the paper. He was gathering information for research he was doing in one of his courses. Within hours of the ad's publication, he began receiving calls. For weeks, he received eighteen to twenty calls a day, and he had run the ad only once. I believe his experiment could be duplicated in any community in any newspaper with the same poignant results. Many people desperately need to be listened to. They frequently pay medical doctors, psychologists, or psychiatrists just to have someone who will listen to them. I believe one of the consequences of not being listened to is to feel personally diminished, unimportant, passed over, and sometimes rejected. These feelings break our spirits, dry our bones, and stifle our laughs.

Though we long to be heard and are thrilled when we find a listening ear, we frequently don't listen in turn. We are often as loath to listen to others as they are to listen to us. With that mind-set no one listens to anyone—we talk—but there are no listeners. Paul Tournier says that conversations between nations, couples, and friends are often merely a dialogue of the deaf. What a tragic commentary this is.

Anton Chekov portrays conversational deafness in the first act of his play, *The Cherry Orchard*. Lyubov, the main character, is coming home from having been away for some time. Everyone is engaged in frenetic activity in preparation for her arrival. The moment Lyubov bursts into the room talking about how wonderful it is to be home, there is instant conversational chaos. Everyone begins talking at once, but no one appears to hear anything anyone else says. Each character is absorbed in his own individual preoccupations.

One woman begins a monologue about the peculiar dietary habits of her dog. Another says she has just received a marriage proposal and has no idea what to do about it since she hardly knows the man. Across the room is heard a complaint about the inconsistency and undependability of the train schedules and the impossibility of getting anywhere efficiently when dependent upon public transportation. Superimposed over all this noise is Lyubov, who is exclaiming to no one in particular how wonderful it is to be home.

If perchance you think Chekov or Tournier are exaggerating a bit, stop and observe your world. When you are with a group of people, notice the conversational patterns. How fully do the people you are observing tune in to what is being said? My good friend Lu Anderson was giving one of her incomparably delicious dinner parties, and as the noise level around her table rose steadily, she burst out laughing, "Oh my goodness, I forgot to invite any listeners." I wonder if finding enough listeners for any event might not prove to be an overwhelming challenge.

Nonlistening patterns are not confined to groups of people; they can be just as obvious on a one-to-one basis. One of the most blatant examples of nonlistening I ever experienced occurred a number of years ago. I was visiting my parents in Cortez, Colorado. It was their custom each summer to retreat from the heat of Phoenix, Arizona, to the wonderfully crisp air of Cortez. Nearly every day my father would enthusiastically pack up his fishing gear, Mother would make a picnic lunch, grab a book, and off they'd go for another day of outwitting the trout. (Mother had no interest in outwitting trout, but she did love sitting under a tree by a sparkling stream and nestling into a good book.) One morning I was asked to fill the car with gas prior to our departure for Trout Lake.

I put the nozzle in the tank, straightened up for a moment and gazed about. The next thing I knew, a woman whom I had never seen before let out a screech of recognition and came galloping across the concrete toward me. She threw her arms around me, clasping me firmly to her ample bosom. "Marlene," she shrieked, "how wonderful to see you." (My admiration for Marlene was enormous as I contemplated the challenge of surviving this woman's hugs.)

"No, I'm afraid I'm not Mar—"

"Oh my dear, imagine meeting here like this after all these years! Now tell me, how are the children?"

"But I really—"

"And your little girl—my goodness—I'll bet she's grown. She must be almost twelve by now. And Elwood! How is Elwood?"

"Please, I . . . " Elwood? Who on earth might Elwood be? He could be a husband, a son, perhaps a pet. In the third grade I think Sharon Abernathy had a possum named Elwood. (He made a most unsatisfactory pet, as I remember.)

"Oh wait 'til my husband finds out I ran into you! He's back at the motel. We were just going to go out for breakfast. Say, why don't you join . . . "

Throughout this encounter I had been trying to interject that I was not Marlene and we did not know each other. Finally, heedless of my attempt to get in a word, she whipped out a pen and paper and without a break in her monologue, she said, "Let me get your phone number. You're undoubtedly staying in a motel here. Wouldn't it be fun if we were in the same one?"

At this point I took a step nearer to her, put my hands on her shoulders, and said, "Wait a minute. I have something to say. I'm not Marlene. We have never met. You don't know me. I don't know Elwood." She stared uncomprehendingly at me for several seconds and then exploded with, "Well, for heaven's sake, why didn't you say so? What a waste of time!"

As I watched her harrumphing her way back to her car, I thought, *Lady, I wanted to say so but you provided no opportunity.* She had tuned me out. She did not listen to me nor care that I had something to say until I forced her to listen.

Shakespeare in *King Henry IV* part 2 says, "It is the disease of not listening, the malady of not marking, I am troubled with." To call not listening a disease and a malady seems very apt to me. A malady is defined as a "disorder, an unwholesome condition." Not only is it a malady to be a nonlistener, but nonlistening produces an unwholesome condition in those who are not heard. My husband witnessed such a malady in Brian, a young man who was Ken's seat partner on a business trip to Boston.

He noted early in the flight that Brian appeared dejected and uncommunicative. Ken felt a desire to make contact with him and possibly be an encouragement. Responding ultimately to the empathy he sensed in Ken,

Brian began to talk. Finally, he talked nonstop. He was failing some of his premed courses; he didn't want to go into medicine; his father would hear of nothing but medicine; his mother didn't care what he did as long as he didn't make her look bad to her friends; no one seemed to care what he wanted to do with his life, at least no one listened to him when he tried to talk about it.

At the conclusion of the five-hour flight, Brian looked at Ken and sheepishly said, "I'm sorry; I've talked nonstop since we left Los Angeles." And then poignantly, he said, "I don't think I've ever had anyone listen to me for five hours straight. In fact, I guess I'm not used to having anyone listen to me at all. I hope you don't mind; I hate to be a bore."

Brian suffered from an unwholesome condition. That condition, that malady, originated in the experience of rarely being heard. As a result he felt apologetic when he found himself talking. He feared being a burden.

I imagine that Brian's father would be shocked at the accusation that he didn't listen to his son. Most people seem unaware that they are not listeners. Because they can repeat a person's words, they assume they have been listening. We have all talked to someone who is rifling through a drawer, sorting magazines, or worse yet, reading the paper. Finally in desperation we say, "You're not listening to me!" The response is, "Of course I'm listening to you—I heard every word you said. You said that you became so exasperated with the car today that you gave it to the Fuller Brush man in exchange for a mop." In triumph the accused says, "See, I heard you!" Yes, he may have heard—but only the words were heard, not the spirit behind them.

We do two types of listening. One is listening for mere facts. With this kind of listening we hear words, process them, and internalize them. This is the kind of listening we do in classes, in business, or in committee meetings. We listen for information. But the kind of listening that most concerns me is what we could call empathetic listening. With this kind of listening we not only hear the facts—the words—but we also hear the heart and the soul behind the words. Brian's father heard the words, but was deaf to his son's heart.

An empathetic listener is a great antidote for someone suffering from a broken spirit and dry bones. I recall times when I have been so ministered to by a friend with the gift of empathetic listening that my broken spirit was mended merely by being heard. I feel loved and affirmed when someone hears my soul. It renews my confidence and restores my peace. It also increases my sense of light-heartedness and my inclination to laugh.

This past winter I was scheduled to speak at a conference in Tucson, Arizona. I was delighted to learn that Ney Bailey was also going to be speaking at this conference. Ney is not only a gifted speaker and writer, she is also one of the most tender and empathetic persons I know. We made plans to take the same flight to Tucson so that we could have some private time together. We hadn't been in the air more than thirty minutes when Ney, with her soft voice and Louisiana inflection, said, "Marilyn, I sense a heaviness in your spirit. Are you really doing all right?" I was a bit startled because to my knowledge I hadn't even hinted that I was feeling troubled. I had received a disturbing phone call before I left home that morning, but I didn't want to impose what I was feeling on Ney. Because we hadn't been together in months, I wanted us to have a good time catching up on each other's lives. I had no intention of unloading on her. But Ney had not only heard my words, she had heard the heart and soul behind them and discerned that my spirit was not at rest.

With her gentle encouragement and probing, I began to open up and reveal the source of my concern. She listened without interruption until I spilled the whole scene to her. When I concluded, I felt something inside me lift. My sense of personal failure seemed less intense and my optimism began to return. As I revealed my soul to Ney, she said very little—but the caring, understanding support I received from her empathetic listening spoke volumes to me. I could feel my joy returning so that, by the time we arrived at our hotel, I felt my spirit mending.

Although we can't make people listen to us, we can at least determine to listen to others. In so doing we can contribute to the healing of broken spirits and dry bones. Let me make a few suggestions that contribute to the art of empathetic listening. First, listen with all of your body.

Turn toward the person speaking and look into his or her eyes, being careful not to let your eyes stray to your surroundings. I've talked to many people whose eyes roam so continuously I wonder what they see and if I should be seeing the same thing since whatever it is, it's a lot more interesting than I am. With your eyes, focus on the person to whom you're listening. Let nothing distract your focus. Stay focused upon them until they have finished speaking. (There are times, I suppose, when adhering steadfastly to this suggestion might prove difficult. I read in the paper this morning about a woman whose car brakes failed. As a result she plowed into the living room of a couple who moments before had been chatting comfortably in their twin rockers. Were I the occupant of one of the rockers, I must confess there would be a strong temptation to avert my eyes from the face of my fellow conversationalist to the car careening toward me from the kitchen.)

Second, don't interrupt. How many times have you expected to have a conversation only to have the other person interrupt you with something like, "I know exactly what you mean. You know, my brother-in-law had an experience like you're describing and just yesterday he said . . ." And they're off and running; the attention never comes back to you. Constant interruption not only destroys the flow of ideas needed to be expressed, it also kills the desire to talk at all. If I'm interrupted continually, I make the assumption that I'm being a bore! Since I don't want to be a bore, I'll stop talking. The desire to express myself is lost; so, too, is my inclination for further conversation with that person.

Third, enter into the mind and the emotion of the person speaking. Perhaps someone shares with you the anguish of his or her recent divorce. As you are listening, imagine what it must feel like to think your marriage is stable and unexpectedly be told your partner wants a divorce. What must it feel like to realize you have to get a job after being out of the public work-world for years? What must it feel like to face family and friends with the news that your marriage has failed? What must it feel like to face the loneliness and insecurity of a future you felt certain was going to be shared with your marriage partner?

Perhaps someone has just experienced the collapse of a business. The dream of a comfortable retirement is replaced with the gnawing fear that even everyday expenses may not be met. How must it feel suddenly to have no financial security? How must that affect the ego of the person whose unwise business decision led to this collapse?

Or maybe what is communicated is no more than a vague dissatisfaction with the day. I saw a bumper sticker that read, "Is today really necessary?" We all wonder at times if today is necessary—that's why we smile at the sticker. But that feeling will pass, another day will come, and more positive emotions will be experienced. For that moment, however, when our daily life seems unnecessary, we need an ear that empathizes with how we feel.

I believe Scripture addresses specifically our need to be heard as well as our need to hear. Galatians 6:2 states, "Bear one another's burdens, and thus fulfill the law of Christ." This verse speaks of reciprocity—I'll bear yours and you bear mine. How can we bear burdens if we don't listen to what those burdens are? In the same vein, Isaiah 61:1 says we are to "bind up the brokenhearted." We can't bind up the brokenhearted if we don't hear what is breaking the heart.

The best definition of empathetic listening I have found is in Romans 12:15: "Rejoice with those who rejoice, and weep with those who weep." When we listen in this manner and feel what the speaker feels, we truly can bear one another's burdens and contribute to the binding up of the brokenhearted.

We Aren't Real

7

Aware of the public's increased demand for authenticity, advertisers are placing an emphasis on the "real thing." We are assured that the cookie we hold in our hand is made with "whole eggs" and "pure dairy butter." Our drinks advertise no artificial sweeteners and our bread contains no preservatives. Even the fabrics we buy assure us they are 100 percent cotton. (I have yet to figure out why 100 percent cotton is such a big deal. My iron and I have huge fights with it at least once a week!)

We all have a basic craving for the real rather than the phony. We love to see people "in the act of being themselves." Why else do *Candid Camera* reruns retain such large viewing audiences? We laugh uproariously when someone is caught without benefit of pretense or cover-up.

More often than not we maintain a veneer of acceptability in our daily lives that belies how we really are. Therefore, we love seeing others without their masks.

Lloyd Ahlem in his book, *Do I Have to Be Me?*, says, "In nonauthentic living, there is a behavioral recipe to know in nearly every social situation." I love that concept—behavioral recipe. How true that we figure out where we are going to be and what is expected of us, and then we follow the approved behavior for that situation.

There is something in me that has often resisted behavioral recipes—resisted to the detriment of my dignity and image. One such time occurred on a Saturday afternoon preceding the beginning of winter semester at Biola. Beth and I drove over to the school so I could put my class syllabuses on the secretary's desk for typing and then distribution to classes Monday morning. I needed to get into my office, but the building was locked on the outside. That meant I had to walk all the way over to the administration building and pick up a master key. I grumbled and snorted my way over there, asked for a key to the building, was told I had to leave my driver's license, agreed to those peculiar terms, made my way back to my office, left the syllabuses, and was irritated that I had to walk all the way back to administration to return the key. Beth had come with me because she had a four o'clock appointment several miles from the university. With all the time involved in tromping across campus for a key, we were in danger of missing her deadline.

At this point I'm going to diverge enormously from the topic but it will fit together ultimately. Since my early twenties I have wanted a Fiat convertible. Prior to falling in love with Ken Meberg, I envisioned myself an old-maid schoolteacher, living in sunny, Southern California, tearing madly through the beach cities in a Fiat convertible. I exchanged that fantasy for the more sedate image of being a married schoolteacher, living in sunny, Southern California, driving sanely through the beach cities in a Ford Falcon. A few years ago, in the midst of my unpredictable midlife years, Ken bought me a gorgeous, blue Fiat convertible. I absolutely loved it! I'd go zipping about in this little machine—my hair flying in all directions—feeling as if I owned the road. I experienced an indescribable sense of euphoria—a touch of reckless abandon—in this little car.

The Biola buildings are connected by a network of sidewalks that crisscross all over the campus. As I walked these various sidewalks during a typical class day, I often mused about the width of the walks and whether or not my Fiat would fit on them—idle ponderings characteristic of a partially vacant mind—nothing more. Now to return to the immediate narrative.

As I walked to the car (my Fiat) to tell Beth that I still had to get the key back to administration and that I feared we would be late for her appointment, a most compelling idea dropped into my head. I looked about the campus. It was nearly four o'clock on a Saturday afternoon, not a sign of life anywhere. The promise of anonymity and sweet fulfillment fueled the idea in my mind. I jumped in the car, backed up carefully, assured myself that Beth and I were the only living creatures within a radius of five miles, and pulled onto the first sidewalk leading to my destination. We were a perfect fit. Just as I was settling into the deliciousness of it all, I heard a jarringly loud honk. I couldn't believe it; there behind me, not on the sidewalk but sitting self-righteously on the road leading to the sidewalk, was a campus security squad car. Where on earth had he come from?

I had almost completed my goal of reaching the steps of the administration building; my presence was now known, my wrongdoing irreversible. Under those circumstances, why stop? So I continued jauntily on my way. The squad car then joined me on the sidewalk. (I was gratified to note in my side mirror that his tires hung over the sides of the walk—it was not a tidy fit at all.) Beth had slipped to the floor of the car in humiliation as the security car's siren and red light came on in response to my heedlessness. Apparently I had stretched my delinquency to the limit. It seemed wise to stop.

To assure the young security man that I was not a fugitive, I hopped out of the car and met him as he got out of his. He stared at me for a moment and then quietly asked, "What are you doing?" I went blank—I didn't really have an answer. I stared vacantly at him. "Why are you driving on the sidewalk? Did you hear me honk? Why didn't you stop?" I didn't have a sensible answer to any of his questions. Looking into his puzzled but warm brown eyes, I ventured, "Well, you probably can't understand this, but you see, I'm in midlife crisis. I get these nearly uncontrollable urges from time to time." He looked at me curiously. "Where were you going?" "Well, actually, I was on my way to the administration building to pick up my driver's license."

I told the officer that I knew my behavior was puzzling as well as reprehensible, that I deserved a citation, and that I would willingly accept one. I had been mentally comforting myself that at least he didn't know who I was. I would take the reprimand and the citation I deserved and quietly leave. He continued to look at me searchingly and finally said, "You're Marilyn Meberg, aren't you? You teach in the English department here—isn't that right?" My heart sank.

He suggested then that I turn around (only I could turn around on the sidewalk—his car was too fat), retrace my steps, park, walk to administration, return the key, and secure my driver's license. An indulgent young man (a Biola graduate student), he did not give me a citation. He did not even give me the scolding I deserved. But he undoubtedly had misgivings about whether I would make it safely through midlife crisis. (I told this incident at a retreat one weekend, and a woman mailed me a bumper sticker which I put on my car. It reads: "If you don't like the way I drive, stay off the sidewalk.")

Now I definitely did not follow the behavioral recipe for navigating the Biola campus. Neither did I follow the behavioral recipe for a faculty member. There are times when it is unwise and even inappropriate not to follow the recipes, and I willingly admit my behavior was unwise. (I don't think I feel much remorse though.) However, if we all follow the various recipes too closely, we become like little cutout figures, looking alike and behaving alike. That kind of conformity is stifling to our spirits; it produces dry bones by robbing us of our uniqueness and individuality. Making sure we are conforming to all the behavioral recipes, looking and behaving like everyone, fearing we may "stick out in a crowd," produces tension. That tension reduces our inclination to relax and have fun.

One of the most refreshing persons I know is a woman who has spent her life in Ecuador as a missionary. Ken and I were at a social gathering one evening where this woman was present. This was my first exposure to her, and I was captivated from the first moment we were introduced. She had none of the stereotyped mannerisms or phrases so common to our image of "missionary." In fact, some of her remarks bordered on the irreverent, but her sincere commitment to her calling and her genuine love of God was unmistakable. After she had gargled, with a throat full of water, a hilarious rendition of "Jesus Loves Me," I asked her privately if some of her antics were criticized by her supporters or coworkers. She laughed heartily and said yes, many people felt she should be less uninhibited, quote Scripture a little more often, and not be so prone to fun and laughter. "But you know," she said, "for years I tried to play a role for my austere missionary father and my subservient mother. To them, serving God was heavy business—little time for fun, little reason for laughter. When I was a child, I was constantly reprimanded for my fun-loving nature; the implication was that sincere piety and lightheartedness didn't mix. When I entered college, one of my Bible professors became my mentor. Through him I began to realize that I was stifling not only who I was but also the God-given gift of fun and spontaneity. He encouraged me to be myself and to recognize my own uniqueness; in essence, he gave me permission to be the person God created me to be. I'll always be grateful to that professor. In fact, it was he whom I first heard gargle 'Jesus Loves Me.' We had to do a skit at a departmental party, and he and I gargled a duet."

This missionary lady with thirty years of service in Ecuador has modeled for me the joy of being released from restricting behavioral recipes. She is different in a wonderfully positive way—she's simply who she is.

There is something exhilarating about variety. Don't you love to see a garden of flowers aglow with myriad colors, shapes, and sizes? The garden would lose much of its appeal if it were all one species, one color, and one shape. Can you imagine a symphony performed only by tubas? We need some tubas, but we need cellos, violins, french horns, clarinets, oboes, drums, cymbals, etc., for a rich, full sound. By the same token, I think we achieve a full, rich sound in life when there is variety among us; when our uniqueness is encouraged so that we make a different sound or look from that of everyone around us.

The inevitable result of rigid conformity is a lack of personal authenticity—a phony rather than real approach to ourselves, to others, and to life's experiences. God did not create any duplicates in nature or humankind. That means I will not always be inclined to behave as everyone else because I am not like anyone else in the world.

Why is it that so many persons are unable to be real or feel uncomfortable about being real? I think for many the freedom to be real was squelched in childhood. As a child grows up, he receives messages about himself that either reinforce his sense of worth or tear it down. Since we all desperately need love and approval, we learn to modify our behavior and responses in order to receive that much-needed affirmation. The child who continually receives negative messages begins to feel he is not acceptable as he is or loved as he is. Therefore, he had better become like someone else who appears to be loved and accepted. I believe at that point the pattern for inauthentic living begins.

Sacrificing personal authenticity to the tyranny of behavioral recipes results in living behind various kinds of masks. Fear of rejection and fear of judgment dictate the masking of who we are, how we feel, and how we think. Anyone who has lived many years behind a mask will testify that it is a lonely place. There are few smiles there—even fewer laughs. Do you remember E. A. Robinson's poem, "Richard Cory?"

Whenever Richard Cory went downtown,
We people on the pavement looked at him:
He was a gentleman from sole to crown,
Clean favored, and imperially slim.
And he was always quietly arrayed,
And he was always human when he talked;
But still he fluttered pulses when he said,
"Good-morning," and he glittered when he walked.
And he was rich—yes, richer than a king—
And admirably schooled in every grace:
In fact, we thought that he was everything
To make us wish that we were in his place.
So on we worked, and waited for the light,
And went without meat, and cursed the bread;
And Richard Cory, one calm summer night,
Went home and put a bullet through his head. [1]

Richard Cory lived behind the mask of attractive affluence and gentlemanly good manners. No one could imagine that behind that façade lived an anguished soul who had lost his impetus to live.

How do we come out from behind the mask? How do we begin the process of becoming real? The psychologist Carl Rogers, in his book *On Becoming Persons*, clarifies a starting point. He says:

As I follow the experience of many clients, in the therapeutic relationship which we create, it seems to me that each one is raising the same question. Below the level of the problem situation about which the individual is complaining, behind the trouble with studies, with wife, or employer, or bizarre behavior, or frightening feelings, lies one central search. It seems to me that at the bottom each person is asking: Who am I, really?[2]

I love the simple profoundness of the ascetic Thomas Merton's response to that question. "My deepest realization of who I am is that I am one loved by Christ." It is the gradual internalizing of that incredible truth that enables us to emerge from behind that which has hidden us from the view of others as well as ourselves. Christ loves me! If Christ loves me, then I must be worthy; I must have merit; I must be more than an OK person. Such a foundation of divine security leads us to necessary further steps, and those steps lead us to each other. It is impossible to become real persons in isolation. We need to be loved, affirmed, and made to feel significant. That is a fact of our relationship with Christ, but we are human creatures who need the human touch as well. Psychiatrist Harry Stack Sullivan says, "Man's need to be closely related to others is as basic as any biological need and, considering the prolonged period of helpless infancy, equally necessary to survival." I believe God ordained our need for one another. Scripture encourages us to love one another, forgive one another, support one another, and, if necessary, lay our lives down for one another.

Carl Rogers lists three conditions that must be present for people if they are to become real:

1. Unconditional acceptance and warmth
2. Empathetic understanding
3. Congruence or genuineness

These are healing qualities. They provide an atmosphere where fear of rejection, fear of judgment, and fear of retaliation are forgotten. In their place we experience the freedom to develop and explore our real selves. When we are accepted, understood, and made to feel genuine caring, we cease to be so hard on ourselves for our flaws and short-comings. Genuine acceptance often provides the inner strength we need to make some changes in ourselves.

Where do we find such a wonderfully healing environment for our growth and development? I would love to say, "It's in the church" or "It's in the midst of our fellow Christians." Unfortunately, that is too often not the case, and that is not the fault of the gospel. The New Testament concept of love is unconditional acceptance, understanding, and genuineness. The frequent inability of the Christian community to replicate that kind of love is a concern to me. Why do we often fail each other in those crucial times of raw hurt and need? I wonder if it is not that we all suffer from essentially the same struggle. We recognize we are not measuring up to that Christlike standard we wish to. There is a battle between who we really are and who Christ calls us to be. We fail to remember not one of us can live up to that standard; it is the risen Christ living his life through us that enables us to accept rather than judge and embrace rather than flee. We need a good shot of the Book of Romans every now and then to remind us that it is not we but Christ. I think we succumb to the lurking suspicion that we are the only ones whose inner person is full of "gunge." We dare not show it, however, and if we hear of anyone else's gunge, we gasp in horror and go running into the streets, renting our clothing. Let's get real! We're all struggling with the same sense of inadequacy and failure from time to time. That's human! Let's minister to each other's hurts and failures, remembering we hurt and fail too. Let's create a climate for one another that can produce growth and change as a result of first experiencing love and support.

Thank God there are wonderful people "out there" to whom we can relate in mutuality and honesty. But you may need to do a bit of searching for them. If at this juncture in your life you think it's worth the search, and you'd love to drop the masks, begin to test the waters for others like yourself. Perhaps you are in a study group right now that could be encouraged to a new level of intimacy and support. Or you may have an existing friendship that, by your example of openness and willingness to be vulnerable, might foster a climate of mutual growth and trust. Go slowly. The majority of persons find it hard to be real with one another because years of masking has become a habit. Psychologist and theorist George A. Kelly warns that "masks have a way of sticking to our faces if worn too long."

One day my phone rang, and the woman on the line identified herself as one who had heard a tape of mine on authenticity. She decided we might enjoy each other so she gave me a call. I discovered she was a speaker and writer herself and that her husband pastored a church in Newport Beach, California. I was flattered, as well as delighted, with the warmth and spontaneity of her overture. Within thirty minutes I was sure I had met one of those rare souls with whom I could be real. Within a few weeks I tested her by saying something I felt was true, but was nevertheless outrageous. There was a slight pause in the conversation, and I was afraid I had offended her when seconds later she said, "Marilyn—I can't believe you said that, but I couldn't agree more. I just wish I could quote you!" I am greatly enriched as this relationship grows and self-disclosure becomes increasingly effortless.

One of the serious consequences of perpetually masking and being phony is that it affects how we relate to God. How many times have we approached the Lord in prayer, careful to put our best spiritual foot forward? It's as if God didn't know that in reality we didn't feel like praying—we'd rather be reading a book, playing tennis, drinking tea, chatting with a friend, or staring at a blank wall. Psalm 51:6 says, "Behold, Thou dost desire truth in the innermost being." God is asking me to approach Him as I am—truthfully, honestly, without a pious mask.

I experienced the refreshment of transparency with him in the midst of one of the major heartbreaks of my life. Our second child, Joanie, was born with very severe spina bifida. We were ignorant of what that birth defect implied. To learn that in all probability Joanie would never walk, have repeated kidney infections, and risk spinal meningitis and perhaps death was overwhelming to us. She looked so perfect (except for the ugly boil-like growth at the base of her spine); she was so helpless, so little; how could all those grim possibilities apply to her?

When the first jolt of shocking reality hit me, I determined that God would heal her. I would not accept any other alternative. I gathered up all my human strength and spiritual understanding of healing, and expected to see God alter the course of our little child's human history.

By the tenth day of Joanie's life, she developed spinal meningitis; on the fifteenth day her fever reached 106 degrees. The doctor called us and said the prognosis for her recovery was minimal. With that news I went into the bedroom, closed the door, and started once again to pray. I praised God for his goodness, for his unfailing mercies, for his Word in which he promised that if we called upon him he would hear us and "show us great and mighty things." I quoted reams of Scripture to him and finally, when I got up off my knees, I thought to myself, *God couldn't help but be impressed with that prayer. I reflected such a vast knowledge of Scripture, and I exhibited a great spirit of faith. He will surely acknowledge the sterling quality of that devotion.* (It is embarrassing to admit, but those truly were my thoughts.) I was convinced that we would be hearing from the doctor soon to say that for reasons that defied his medical knowledge and expectations, Joanie's temperature had dropped and that his fear of brain damage had not been realized.

I wasn't prepared when, several hours later, the doctor called to say that Joanie had just died. I held the phone to my ear in disbelief. How could that be—I had just prayed an exemplary prayer. Joanie was supposed to be healed! How could she have died?

After Ken and I had cried together, talked, and cried some more, I returned to the bedroom to pray. Once again I thanked God for his goodness, for his mercies—but the words began to stick in my throat. What was good or merciful about the birth and death of a little child who had no say over the condition into which she entered the world? What good were all those great promises about healing if God didn't honor them? For the first time in fifteen days, I became real with God. I dropped my phony mask of affected piety and poured out all my confusion and hurt; confessed my faltering faith in his love and goodness; and cried out for a sense of his presence which had eluded me since Joanie's birth. My soul felt dry and parched.

Gradually, with all my anger and hurt honestly expressed, God began to heal my soul. I saw myself as he saw me: one who was frightened but refused to admit it; one who had attempted to win God's favor with her spiritual prowess; one who refused to allow God's sovereign will if it went contrary to her own.

That was the woman God had seen all the time—not the one behind the mask of unflinching faith and strength. It was the tired one to whom God said, "Come to me, all who are weary and heavy-laden, and I will give you rest" (Matthew 11:28). God gave me rest, but not until I communicated to him "truth in my innermost being." When I came out from behind my mask, approached God as the shaken, insecure, and doubting person I truly was, I experienced the sweetness of Isaiah 66:13, "As one whom his mother comforts, so I will comfort you."

I still do not understand the why of Joanie's brief little life; there is much I do not understand about divine healing, but I do have much more peace in not knowing than I once did. I also have an appreciation for the imperative of coming to God with an honest heart rather than a mask. God doesn't minister to the phony front. He sees behind our masks, and he longs to love, comfort, and sustain us. We need to be real with him.

We Aren't Forgiving

8

For a number of years, I was a sandbox "lurker." While our children were growing up, I would lurk about their sandbox, eavesdropping. Conversations were fairly easy to pick up because the sandbox was located just off the patio outside the family room. I could position myself in a chair near the open doors and hear perfectly. Sometimes I would dust and polish the furniture in that part of the room. (To be a successful "lurker" one must not be discovered; engaging in what appears to be meaningful activity is essential!) I loved hearing my preschoolers and their friends talking unguardedly about themselves, each other, and their general perceptions of the world. The relaxed and unstructured atmosphere of the sandbox seemed to inspire some rather weighty exchanges. I didn't want to miss any of them.

One afternoon our son, Jeff, said to his friend Tommy, "Do you think Diane's mom has a crabby face?" Tommy, who was two years older than Jeff and rarely at a loss for an answer to the complexities of life, was silent for a moment. During that interval Diane's mother's face came before me, and I decided that yes, she really did have a crabby face. Tommy's response was uncharacteristically slow in coming. Finally he said, "Yeah, she's got a crabby face, but she's got crabby stuff in her. Some moms have crabby stuff and some don't." Jeff's generous response was, "Well, your mom doesn't have crabby stuff." Tommy paused again and finally said "I know—but sometimes your mom does." I left my post at the window to go clean the garage.

I'm afraid Tommy hit upon a painful truth. A lot of us have crabby stuff in us, and that stuff inevitably shows on our faces. Unresolved anger often surfaces in irritability. Everyone has a problem with anger—even if it's only because we are on the receiving end. Unresolved anger can be an enormous contributor to the breaking of our spirits and the drying of our bones, but this emotion can be dealt with in such a way that smiles squelched by anger can return.

I have often heard people deny they even have feelings of anger. They claim to be occasionally "irritated" or "ticked off," but never angry. To allow oneself actually to

feel anger could, in the minds of many, be to allow oneself to sin.

It is essential to recognize that anger itself is not wrong.
Our angry feelings can be legitimate; it is our response to
that anger that may not be. Dr. David Seamonds, psychologist to the staff and students of Asbury College and
Seminary, expresses what is common to the thinking of
many Christians:

> I grew up on some unbiblical, inhuman, and destructive
> preaching about anger always being an unsanctified emo-
> tion. It took me years to get over these attitudes. They
> almost destroyed my Christian life and nearly wrecked
> my marriage, because I had to learn how to properly
> express my anger to my wife. Every good husband or wife
> has to learn how to do that in acceptable ways.[1]

Anger is an emotion; it is a feeling, not a behavior. We
cannot place a value judgment upon feelings; they simply
are. However, our feelings can lead either to right or
wrong behavior. Our feelings can also lead either to right
attitudes or wrong attitudes. We have a choice about how
we behave after we become angry, and we are responsible
for those choices and the resultant behavior.

The Bible speaks of anger frequently. God is reported
as being angry several hundred times in the Old Testament.
But God's anger is a justifiable and righteous reaction to
the unrighteousness of his creation. However, God's

anger is not removed from his nature of love. Psalm 103:8 states "The LORD is compassionate and gracious, slow to anger and abounding in lovingkindness."

A prominent Old Testament figure who exhibited anger was Moses. When he came down from the mountain, having received the Ten Commandments from God, and found the Israelites singing and dancing in idol worship, Moses threw the tablets down, breaking them to pieces. Moses' anger at the people's ungodliness went without scriptural condemnation. But there was another occasion when God did condemn the anger of Moses. The Israelites were in need of water; they were doing their usual griping and complaining. The pressure was getting to Moses. God told him to "speak to the rock" and water would come forth for all the people. But Moses, in his human frustration, did not follow God's instructions. Instead of speaking to the rock, he hit it. Water came forth, but God reprimanded Moses for his angry disobedience. In the throwing down of the tablets, Moses' anger was righteous indignation at the ungodliness of his people. In the second instance, Moses allowed his frustration to be expressed in preference to the divine command. For that, Moses was rebuked by God. However, in neither case is the feeling of anger scripturally addressed, only the behavior resulting from the anger.

We read in the New Testament that Jesus was frequently angry with those who opposed him as he went about relieving oppression, injustice, and physical suffering. Mark 3:5

says Jesus looked at them "with anger" as the Pharisees attempted to prevent the Sabbath healing of the man with a withered hand. And of course, Jesus' anger was most obvious as he threw the moneychangers out of the temple.

Paul writes more about anger than anyone in the New Testament. Most interesting to me is his statement in Ephesians 4:26, "Be angry, and yet do not sin." This implies that anger itself can become sin if it is not dealt with constructively.

Anger is a natural, involuntary, physiological response to personal threat or harm, and therefore can be a positive emotion. Anger can motivate us to work against the many social ills of society. If one becomes sufficiently angry at the injustices of the world and then mobilizes that anger-induced energy to work for social change, human suffering can be greatly lessened.

A number of years ago a dear friend of mine accompanied me on a weekend retreat where I was speaking. On our way home we decided to stop and indulge in a huge piece of "home-baked apple pie" covered with vanilla ice cream. (Our decision was not justified by the expediency of a flat tire or need of gas—we had to admit openly to a gluttonous motivation.)

The restaurant we chose was full, so we opted to stand in line at a little side window for take-out pie and ice cream. Behind us was a woman who loudly and continuously berated a little girl who I assumed was her daughter. Apparently the girl had been responsible for the whereabouts of her younger brother. She had lost track of him momentarily, and her mother was furious. She called the little girl "stupid" and "irresponsible" and claimed the child had ruined the only day off the mother had had in weeks. The girl was visibly embarrassed by her mother's accusations since they were stated with sufficient volume to be heard for a city block.

As our pie was handed to us, the wayward little boy ran up to his mother and sister, excitedly telling them about the "petting farm" he had discovered on the property and that he had been petting a goat. The mother ordered pie for herself and the two children. Just as I thought the tension was easing within the mother, she shouted, "You little brat—what do I care about you petting a goat?" With that she slapped him so hard across the side of the face, his pie went flying into the dirt and he staggered to his knees.

A Vesuvius-like emotion had been building steadily in me since this woman's diatribes first assaulted my ears in the pie line. When the little boy's head snapped around from the slap on the face and his pie hit the dirt, I could stand it no longer. I bounded across the distance between us in a second, and as the woman raised her hand for the second slap, I grabbed her wrist and hissed, "You touch that child and you'll have the law to deal with." She glowered at me for a moment or two and then abruptly turned and walked away. What broke my heart as I looked at the little boy still on his knees was that I could do nothing to prevent the slaps that he would undoubtedly receive in the future. I offered him my untouched pie; he shook his head no and slowly followed his mother. I was sick for hours afterward; I still get tears in my eyes as I see his little face in my mind.

I will have to admit that I felt an unholy, murderous impulse toward that woman. In fact, I think if she had struck the child again, I might have knocked her teeth out. If I had, my anger would have ceased to be a positive emotion; it would have become an aggressive, inexcusably hostile action. We never have biblical license to attack aggressively either with our actions or our words. The distinction between aggression and anger is crucial to our understanding of anger.

Aggression is a behavior intended to threaten or injure the security of its victim. If I had allowed my anger to become aggression, I would have been as sinfully guilty as the mother.

Because anger frequently produces more negative responses than positive, it is an emotion that is often denied by Christians. This denial results in an unhealthy sublimating of anger. The feelings are pushed below the surface of either expression or consciousness, and a most ungodly emotion then takes over: resentment. Resentment is repressed anger that usually smolders and ultimately seeks revenge. This emotion leads to an often subtle but usually concrete attack on others. If it is not turned on others, it is often turned inward against our own body.

A most graphic description of the effects of resentment is expressed by the black American poet Langston Hughes.

What happens to a dream deferred?
Does it dry up like a raisin in the sun? Or fester like a sore—
And then run?
Does it stink like rotten meat?
Or crust and sugar over—
like a syrupy sweet?
Maybe it just sags
like a heavy load.
Or does it explode?[2]

When resentment is allowed to fester within us, we inevitably experience the physical consequences. Medical research has revealed that the connection between our emotions and our body processes is closely related. Resentment eats away at our insides in much the same way acid would. For example, if I take something Ken says to me as an insult, I will experience anger which becomes hurt. If I do not deal positively with that hurt, it will probably grow into resentment toward him. Every time I think about what he said (that I perceived to be an insult), I am going to experience again the feeling of hurt and resentment. Each time I feel that hurt, my body prepares to do something about it—it becomes readied for action. If I fail to do anything to neutralize my hurt, my body becomes readied time after time. After a while, it will react under the strain of a continual state of preparedness that does not result in resolving my hurt. Many physical ailments such as headaches, stomach problems, colitis, and hypertension are nothing more than suppressed anger that has been translated into resentment.

St. Augustine said, "Anger is a weed; hate is the tree." Do I dare have the audacity to disagree with St. Augustine? I suggest that anger is not the weed, resentment is the weed; and, if nurtured and cultivated by our minds, it will develop into tree-size hatred. Obviously, we all need to find ways to deal with anger so that resentment is not given space to take root and break our spirits.

To begin with, we must acknowledge that we experience anger and recognize it will soon be translated into aggression, resentment, or even hatred if we don't deal with it. In order to deal with it, we need to understand it. Why is anger present? What occasions that white-hot flash? What is its source? We need to bring anger before us and submit it to close scrutiny.

This requires that we observe ourselves closely; listen sensitively to our emotions. Let me cite an example.

Several years ago I was speaking at a women's retreat in another state. As the music and other preliminaries were going on prior to my first presentation, I idly scanned the audience. To my surprise, a woman I had known years ago in California was sitting in the front row. She met my gaze, nodded coldly, and looked away. Her response made me feel uncomfortable, but I shrugged it off. My topic for that evening was unconditional love. The women were extremely receptive as I spoke, and I warmed inwardly. At the conclusion of that meeting many women came up to me, telling me how helpful my comments were to them; how illuminating it was to realize how subtly they were demanding performance first and granting love second, etc. As I was privately fanning the embers of my obnoxious ego, the woman whom I had known in California stepped in front of me and said, "It's a bit ironic to hear you speak so convincingly about unconditional love." With that, she turned abruptly and walked away.

That night I thrashed around in my bed remembering that woman's words and the anger they produced in me. I acknowledged my anger, but I felt perfectly justified in my feelings. I refused to think deeply about why her words had such an effect on me—I chose to remain at the level of thinking that assured me I had legitimate cause for anger.

The next morning I was to speak on forgiveness. Again, many women came up afterward and shared stories from their own lives and how they felt a new desire to have a forgiving spirit. Predictably, the woman from California waited her turn and stepped directly in front of me with another caustic remark. "I imagine it's much easier to speak on these topics when you're several states away from home, isn't it?" Again, she turned abruptly and walked away. I maintained my "retreat speaker" demeanor throughout the lunch that followed the morning session. But as soon as I got back to my room, I flounced from chair to chair in an effort to come to terms with my negative emotions.

Almost ten years prior to this retreat, I had been a guest at a luncheon where this woman was also a guest. As that luncheon progressed, the topic of divorce among Christians came up. Soon everyone was talking about the divorce of a particular Christian leader. I had been having a difficult time during this discussion because I think divorce, Christian or non-Christian, is a shattering experience, and I am deeply troubled that we too often focus on the failure of the divorced persons rather than the loving rehabilitation of their psyche and spiritual well-being. When this woman stated that divorced persons should be expelled from the church and all relationship with them severed, I could remain silent no longer. I turned to her and said I found her legalism nauseating and her lack of Christian charitability repugnant. Of course a pall settled over the room; the subject was nervously changed to something safe like the rejuvenating effect of adding aspirin to the water in which cut flowers are placed.

For a while I entertained the notion that I should call her and apologize. Though I did find that woman's spirit repugnant, I had no right to embarrass her in front of others. It was a most ungracious comment for me to make no matter how justified I might have felt in making it. But I never seemed to get around to calling her. Time passed; I heard she had moved, and I never thought of her again. And here she was now, sitting stonily in the front row at this retreat.

Fidgeting in my room, I seriously began to analyze my emotions. Her comments had struck an exposed nerve. She was right; it was a lot easier to wax eloquent about unconditional love several states away. No one knows that I don't always live up to what I say. She was also right in her implication that there was irony in my talking about unconditional love. This woman had been the object of anything but my unconditional love. She had exposed me to myself; I didn't like what I suspected to be true, so instead of owning up to my own repugnance, I scapegoated my emotion to her and comforted myself by saying my anger was justified.

Of course this self-revelation brought the inevitable response—I resented her. Why should she suddenly drop into my life, staring at me from the front row? I knew I was not a consistent example of what I was talking about, but I didn't want to admit that to her! And yet, I had to. I had to apologize for the hurt I had inflicted upon her and make restitution.

With reluctance, I located her room and asked if we could go for a walk. She woodenly reached for her sweater and followed me wordlessly out the door. I told her about the anger I was experiencing from her remarks, but that I realized what she was implying with them was absolutely true. I then sincerely apologized for my lack of kindness at the luncheon years ago. I told her that my lack of compassion for her feelings in front of the group was inexcusable, and, swallowing the lump of pride that kept filling my throat, I asked for her forgiveness. When she didn't say anything and merely continued walking beside me, I looked closely at her for some response. To my amazement I saw tears spilling down her cheeks.

After a while she began to talk. She told me when she saw the retreat brochure with my name and picture on it, she determined to come to undermine me and make me feel uncomfortable. Resentment had eaten at her all those years because of my intemperate remark at the luncheon. She further explained that she herself had been divorced at an early age and that her pastor father had virtually disowned her because of the embarrassment she had caused him. Instead of gaining compassion from her experience, she became bitter and was determined that others would suffer as much as she had. I was totally stricken by her revelation as she detailed her anguish: a sense of alienation from her father, whom she resented but still desperately sought to please; a conviction that God not only disapproved of her but withheld his love from her as well; and a burden of playing the role of Christian while seething inside with feelings of bitterness and resentment. For the first time I understood her behavior, and I hurt for her. I put my arms around her, and we sobbed for several minutes. In the time remaining at the retreat we took every opportunity to be alone together and to talk. Our spirits were healed as a result of the candid hours we spent together. She forgave me for my insensitivity and saw me with eyes now unclouded by resentment.

I learned some invaluable lessons from this experience. To analyze my anger to determine its source is imperative, but it is not enough. I must neutralize my anger so that it does not become resentment. Since anger is nearly always in response to another human being, it can be neutralized by open, honest, nonaggressive communication with the person who hurt us. If my friend and I had not confronted each other and talked, our anger would not have been neutralized.

Dr. Theodore Rubin in *The Angry Book* uses the unexpected phrase "warm anger." By this he means that though one feels anger there is no "vindictiveness, sadism, or vengeful purpose" in communicating those feelings. Warm anger shows respect for the other person and a willingness to hear his feelings. It does not mean there are no strong words used in the exchange, but warm anger insists on words that will in no way involve "physical force, coercion, or brutality." Dr. Rubin goes on to say:

All expressions of warm anger will be short, finite; they will not go on and on and become chronic. There will be no grudge-carrying of slush accumulation. Angry feelings will be short-lived—finished, over with—and will be followed by forgiving and forgetting if appropriate. The expression of warm anger will have a cleansing effect on the relationship. It will clear the air of cobwebs of confusion, hurt feelings, and misunderstandings.[3]

If our anger can be "warmly" communicated and "warmly" received, then the path is cleared to get to the root of the problem, which is, why did we become angry in the first place? Communicating anger is only the beginning step in healing the acid-wounds that anger has induced. The real task begins when we seek to determine causes and cures.

If confrontation seems to be too great a risk, then anger must be neutralized some other way. There are a number of methods I find helpful for those times when I decide confrontation is too risky. One is simply to pace the floor and talk out loud. Everything that is in my head and heart is audibly verbalized. The intent of this is not to try to talk myself into any particular position; it is merely to get my thoughts out, and for me to hear them fully. This helps to calm me, plus it brings clarity. Sometimes I can see my own contribution to the problem, and with that altered perspective I can seek to remedy what I'm responsible for.

In a similar vein, there is release that comes from writing a letter to the person for whom I feel negative emotion. The key to the success of this exercise is that I write out everything I think and feel. I hold nothing back, but I don't mail it! The exercise is for me—not the person I'm writing to. Often, on reading the letter several hours later, I find myself feeling much more charitable and far less resentful. Another excellent release from anger is crying. Tears can cleanse away many of the impurities that poison the system.

The suggestions in the previous paragraphs can be helpful, but I think they are merely first-aid treatments to tide us over until true healing can occur. True healing comes with true forgiveness, and true forgiveness occurs only as we seek God's aid. Many times I resist God's aid because I don't want to forgive. To forgive would let the person, whom I perceive to be in the wrong, off the hook, and I don't feel he deserves to be off the hook! But neither do I deserve that ripped-up feeling I have inside from allowing my resentment to fester, nor do I want the spiritual estrangement I experience when I choose to nurture my grievance. God clearly commands that I forgive others as he has forgiven me. There's no way to get around it: forgive or fester.

How do we begin the process of forgiving? We begin where we are. If your resentment is still so strong you don't really want to let go of it but you know you should, acknowledge to God that that is where you are. Then go one step further: "I'm not willing to let go of my resentment, but I'm willing to be made willing." Though this may seem to be a small step, it's a crucial one because nothing moves ahead until we, with deliberate act of the will, determine that we will be obedient to God's command. God can then begin to work to soften our spirit and to alter and shape our attitudes.

At this point God often reminds me of some of the reasons why the offending person said or did what he did. When I become empathetic and literally put myself in the other person's world and walk in his shoes, my spirit inevitably softens. That softened state makes me receptive to God's Spirit, who encourages me to forgive. As I pray, I pray for God's forgiveness for myself and my resentful attitudes. I also pray that God will, with his supernatural power, heal me of my resentment. I don't believe it's possible to forgive sincerely without the enabling power of God. Once I have covenanted with God that I do want to experience healing, I claim it as an accomplished fact and, in partnership with God, seek to restructure my thought patterns so that the old resentment is not allowed to take up residence within me again.

Anger must be neutralized before it destroys you. Anger is the antithesis of joy. You hardly need me to remind you that if you're full of angry resentment, you will not be full of joy. The two emotions cannot live together. Living with the by-products of anger takes enormous energy. I don't believe it is possible to expend energy for much else. If that's the case, unless anger is neutralized, joy and laughter will be rare experiences. Joy can come when we express our anger constructively, when we work consistently at neutralizing resentment, and when we forgive.

Let me close this chapter with the rest of the story about my friend. In the years that have passed since the retreat we have become very good friends. With the gentle understanding and compassionate help of a Christian counselor, she has learned to deal with the anger and resentment spawned by her father's rejection. The purging of that anger and the healing of those memories has transformed her manner. Though she remains a quiet, often shy person, there is a far greater inclination to smile and laugh than there ever was before. Her delight in humor and her frequent smile are a dramatic change from the frozen unresponsiveness so characteristic of her earlier.

We were having lunch several months ago and found ourselves distracted as well as amused by the peculiar antics of a woman several tables away. Apparently she could not find a position at her table that was comfortable for her. We watched, fascinated, as she moved the other chairs away from the table so that she could move her chair around it inch by inch. Every few minutes she would move her chair a few inches to the right until she had made a complete circle around the table. Apparently she found no agreeable spot because she stalked out—but not until she grabbed the basket of rolls and dumped them into her purse. My friend's comment was, "I wonder why she didn't butter them first!" As our lunch progressed, I forgot about the woman until I realized my friend was moving her chair every now and then until she had circled the table and was a few inches away from me. We both laughed when I finally caught on to what she was doing—and I was refreshed as I recognized in my friend an inclination for fun and an enjoyment of life's oddities. Her joy had returned.

We Aren't Content

Five years ago I hit that much talked about, greatly-dreaded milestone—my fortieth birthday! Early in our marriage Ken and I determined to have fun when it was legitimate and laugh if it were possible. Therefore, rather than drape the house in black, mourning my lost youth, Ken gave me a party like none I've ever experienced! He invited eighteen of our favorite friends to dress in their best finery and meet at our house for a night of celebration. I only knew we were dressing "to the teeth" and Ken was hosting dinner at some great restaurant.

Ken is extremely creative and a gourmet cook. He loves to "doo-dink" about the kitchen occasionally, producing mouth-watering delicacies fit for the photo centerfold of *Gourmet* magazine. He created a gorgeous platter of hors d'oeuvres complete with deviled quail eggs and caviar. (I have yet to reach the level of sophistication where I can swallow instead of gag when eating caviar, but the idea was fun!) As everyone arrived, they sang and shouted encouragement about my aged state and dove enthusiastically into Ken's fabulous tray of hors d'oeuvres.

In the midst of all this preliminary hilarity, Luci Swindoll and Pete Kling rose to their feet, and in beautiful harmony began solemnly singing, "Marilyn's forty, Marilyn's forty" to the tune of the chorus "Alleluia." Ken picked up their key on the piano, and at a funereal tempo the entire group joined in repetitiously singing forty lines of "Marilyn's forty." If it were not that my mental health is fairly good, I might have cracked then and there at their somber and personalized rendition of what used to be one of my favorite choruses. They assured me that my day really had come and gone and from now on I would live my life primarily in the misty world of memory.

We took off for dinner in three cars with Ken and me in the lead. I was quietly anticipating the fun as well as the ambiance of several gorgeous restaurants Ken might choose. I love to be surprised, so not knowing where we were going contributed to the excitement. We pulled into the parking lot of a little drive-in hamburger joint whose clientele were those generally a bit down on their luck. Stretched across the front of this restaurant was a thirty-foot sign that read, "Happy Birthday, Marilyn." Stunned, but also tickled at Ken's ingenuity, I joined the others as we stormed into the place and took our seats at the tables securely grounded into the concrete floor. On each of the twelve tables was a lone candle, most of which had seen brighter days and all of which I recognized as belonging to me. Ken enthusiastically shouted out our order: eighteen cheeseburgers, eighteen orders of french fries, eighteen Cokes and eighteen packets of ketchup. I loved it! What a far cry from what I had expected! Here we were, looking terribly respectable in our good clothes, slurping Cokes, and chomping down cheap hamburgers.

After several more mournful renditions of "Marilyn's forty," we piled back in the cars and headed for our house for games and presents. (You would never believe some of those presents!) While we were stopped at a light, fully assured by my friends that I was over the hill, I jumped out of the car and ran over to the main street onto which we were all waiting to turn and stuck out my thumb. I was curious to see if, in my aged state, I would be offered a ride. I looked back at my friends in their cars; everyone was laughing. Within seconds, a filthy, utterly disreputable-looking pickup truck with a beat-up, old motorcycle in the back came screeching to the curb and stopped. The driver and his truck were a perfect match. He stretched a grimy hand across to the passenger door, opened it, and leaning across the seat said, "You want a ride, sweetie?" Experiencing a mild sense of alarm, I looked back at the frozen looks of disbelief on the faces of my friends and simply could not resist.

With the strains of "Marilyn's forty" ringing in my ears, I hopped into the filthy cab, slamming the door behind me. As we lurched away from the curb, my chauffeur cast a sidelong glance at me and said, "You don't look like the type of chick who hitchhikes." I quickly assured him that I was not the type of "chick" who hitchhiked, and I asked if he'd be willing to do me a favor. I explained that it was my fortieth birthday and that we had all just finished eating hamburgers at George's. He looked at me in surprise and asked, "Are you Marilyn?" Equally surprised I said, "Well, yes, how did you know?" He told me he had been planning to stop and get a hamburger but was scared off by all the people inside the restaurant. Then he noticed the happy birthday sign and assumed he'd be interrupting a party if he came in. I told him that all evening my friends had been telling me I was past my prime and just to assure them I hadn't lost my incredible magnetism, would he drive me home? He asked if I wouldn't like to go somewhere first for more celebrating. I thanked him for his generosity but assured him that my husband, children, and some friends were in the car directly behind him, and the car to his immediate left, as well as the car directly in front of him were all from my party. It appeared his truck was well-flanked for my protection. He laughed and promised to play it straight and that he'd be happy to drive me home.

We had a marvelous conversation during that ten-minute drive to my house. He declared that I was a "classy-looking broad" and wanted to know if I worked. I didn't want to tell him I taught English at Biola University because I thought somehow word of one of the school's female faculty members hitchhiking a ride home might not be a positive image for the school. However, he did manage to extract that information from me. He was aware of Biola and knew of its fine Christian standards. His entire demeanor changed with that knowledge, and he began to tell me about himself and what a disappointment he was to his parents. He had always wanted to achieve more in his life, but it seemed that nothing ever worked out for him. He told me about his recent divorce, what a hurt it was that the courts had not given him custody of his son, and what a failure he felt himself to be.

As we pulled up to my driveway, he concluded by saying, "You know, every day I tell myself I'm going to do something worthwhile with my life, and every day I don't do it. I've tried different jobs and haven't liked any of them. I've been married twice and haven't been happy. I know I drink too much. I don't seem to know what to do with myself or my life. I want more, but I don't know how to get it or where to find it. All I know is what I got isn't what I want." I was deeply touched by the sense of pathos that accompanied this young man's personal revelations. It was all I could do to keep from reaching over and hugging him. However, my party had all arrived and I knew they, and especially Ken, would be understandably unreceptive to such a gesture. Instead, I shook his hand and thanked him for participating in my "revenge." I also told him that strange as this experience was, I felt it was for a purpose. I urged him to begin reading the Gospel of John and to get in touch with the God who loved him and created him. He didn't verbally respond to what I said, but his expression was very soft as he turned away.

The image of that young man and his sense of disillusionment and searching has hung in my mind ever since. His description of his life reminds me of Matthew Arnold's depressing evaluation of what he considers the typical life experience.

> Most people eddy about here and there, Eat and drink, chatter and love and hate, Gather and squander, are raised aloft, Are hurled in the dust, Striving blindly, achieving nothing: And then they die.[1]

To me, the most chilling line in this excerpt is "striving blindly, achieving nothing." Despite all that human expenditure of energy, the strivings ultimately mean nothing and are merely followed by death. Admittedly, Arnold's depiction of "most people" is not very positive, but I can't help but believe there is much truth in what he says.

Though the strivings of humankind are many and varied, I'd like to narrow our considerations for this chapter to an examination of three arenas in which I believe the majority of persons strive.

I believe all of us have experienced the striving for possessions. It is an odd fact of human nature that we are rarely satisfied with what we have; we always want more. Do you remember how wonderful you thought it would be when you could finally afford to buy the house you wanted so desperately? With the possessing of the house and the passing of time, that house became either too small, too large, too far from work, or too engulfed by crabgrass. The car that was so luxurious now doesn't seem to have nearly as smooth a ride, and certainly the design of the newer model is more appealing than the old. The raise in salary has been slurped up somewhere and another raise would secure a much better financial position. The list goes on and on.

A number of years ago Ken and I reveled in an excellent show put on by Georgia Brown at the Westwood Playhouse in Los Angeles. She told her audience that as a little girl she dreamed of being a famous singer. Along with fame, she dreamed of cars, furs, men, and money; she wanted it all. One afternoon she was in her recording studio idly chatting with her songwriter, and she mentioned how as a child she'd always dreamed of the very possessions she now had. She was amazed that somehow they didn't seem very important once achieved; they didn't produce the satisfaction she had anticipated. She looked at him then and asked, "Is this all there is?"

That afternoon her songwriter called and said he had written a song based on their morning conversation and could he come over and show it to her. He had entitled it, "Is That All There Is?" Georgia heard it, shrugged her shoulders, and turned it down as a song she might record—it was too personal. When Peggy Lee recorded that song, it was a monumental hit and became one of her trademark numbers. Georgia said few people know that song was originally written for her as an expression of her disillusionment with the world of "things."

The writer of the Old Testament book Ecclesiastes testifies to the futility of striving after possessions. He confesses that he built great houses, gardens, and parks for himself. He had flocks and herds far greater than anyone else's, and multitudes of male and female slaves to see that everything was well managed. His treasury of silver and gold far exceeded that of anyone else. He says, "and all that my eyes desired I did not refuse them. I did not withhold my heart from any pleasure" (2:10). He concludes the recounting of his vast number of possessions and indulgences with these rather haunting words: "Thus I considered all my activities which my hands had done and the labor which I had exerted, and behold, all was vanity and striving after wind and there was no profit under the sun" (2:11).

Throughout history many people have concluded that fulfillment and joy do not come with the acquiring of possessions whether those possessions are tangible as are houses, cars, and boats, or intangible as are prestige, power, and fame. Leo Tolstoy, at the height of his literary power and worldwide acclaim wrote in *My Confession*:

> I felt the ground on which I stood was crumbling, that there was nothing for me to stand on, that what I had been living for was nothing; that I had no reason for living . . . . To stop was impossible, to shut my eyes so that I couldn't see that there was nothing in my future but ultimate death.[2]

Tolstoy then began an exhaustive search for truth—for meaning to his existence that would quell the growing fear that his life was nothing and that he had no reason for living.

I believe Tolstoy's experience parallels that of many who realize there must be more to life than simply acquiring or even achieving. Why are we here? What is our purpose? Does anything really make sense? Driven by such questions one then enters another arena of striving—that of bringing philosophical or theological order out of the chaos in which we live.

Literature, especially twentieth-century writings, reflects this struggle to find meaning in life. The futility of striving for cosmic sense is a frequent theme. The old waiter in Ernest Hemingway's short story, "A Clean, Well-Lighted Place," illustrates this viewpoint. At the end of the story he climbs into bed late at night, saying to himself:

"What did he fear? It was not fear or dread. It was a nothing which he knew too well. It was all a nothing and a man was nothing too." And then because he has experienced the death of God he goes on to recite the Lord's Prayer in blasphemous despair: "Our Nothing who art in Nothing, nothing be thy nothing."

In Sartre's novel *Nausea*, Roquentin is walking in the city park one day. Suddenly, he is overcome by the nausea of the meaninglessness of life. Looking around him, he concludes, "Every existent is born without reason, prolongs itself out of weakness and dies by chance." He was forced to the unhappy conclusion that the key to life is its fundamental absurdity. Man as man has to reach toward being God in order to fulfill his aspirations, yet with God dead and the world as it is, these aspirations are limitations cast back in his face as an absurdity. Sartre's reluctant conclusion is that "man is a useless passion."

Shakespeare has Macbeth render one of the bleakest soliloquies in all of literature.

> Life's but a walking shadow, a poor player
> That struts and frets his hour upon the stage
> And then is heard no more. It is a tale
> Told by an idiot, full of sound and fury,
> Signifying nothing.

If life is merely a tale told by an idiot which signifies nothing, there ceases to be reason to strive for meaning. Significance, then, comes only through the experiences of the senses. In other words, "if it feels good, do it" or "eat, drink and be merry for tomorrow we die." If possessions don't seem to satisfy and life makes little sense, there's always the diversions of the heart and body to occupy us. We then begin another striving searching for that love that will provide emotional and physical fulfillment.

Probably the most visible playing out of this scenario can be seen among some Hollywood celebrities. Saturated with everything that money can buy, many seek to fill the void with one love affair after another. These affairs often result in marriage and the sure conviction that the current partner is "everything I've been looking for." Unfortunately, in a few months or possibly years, we learn that the much-publicized romance has gone bad and the two lovers have separated only to begin the search once again.

When Roberta Flack, in her rich, sonorously dusky tones, sings a love song, I invariably get layers of goose bumps. I am especially stirred by her incomparable rendering of "The First Time Ever I Saw Your Face." Some lines in that song speak to the universality of our quest for ultimate fulfillment:

> *The first time ever I lay with you*
> *And felt your heart beat close to mine*
> *I thought our joy would fill the earth*
> *And last till the end of time.**

*THE FIRST TIME EVER I SAW YOUR FACE by Ewan MacColl © Copyright 1962 (renewed) by STORMKING MUSIC INC. All rights reserved. Used by permission.

The songwriter states that this love will last "till the end of time." Everyone hopes to find that one, never-before-experienced love that will last forever.

Literature faithfully mirrors every element of life, and much of it reflects the varied hurts of the heart. In Leo Tolstoy's classic *Anna Karenina*, we are mesmerized and horrified as we watch the beautiful and seemingly unattainable Anna slowly succumb to the overtures of the handsome but shallow Vronsky. As she makes the ill-fated decision to leave her respectable but machinelike husband, we feel relief tinged with fear for her future with Vronsky and his history of self-indulgence. Anna discards all respectability by leaving her husband and her much adored young son to live with Vronsky in Europe. Several months later, Vronsky is seated by himself at a little sidewalk cafe. Tolstoy reveals to the reader Vronsky's thoughts:

> Vronsky, in spite of the complete realization of what he had so long desired, found that he was not perfectly happy. He soon felt that the realization of his desires gave him no more than a grain of sand of the mountain of happiness he had expected. It showed him the mistake people make in picturing to themselves happiness as the realization of their desires. For a time after joining his life to hers, he had felt all the delight of freedom in his love— and he was content, but not for long. He was soon aware that there was springing up in his heart a dissatisfaction—

a weariness. Without conscious intention, he began to clutch at every passing caprice.[3]

Vronsky's growing dissatisfaction was equaled only by Anna's feelings of guilt at leaving her son, and her neurotic insecurity that she would lose Vronsky's love. The story ends in tragedy.

Psychiatrist Scott Peck, in his excellent book, *The Road Less Traveled*, states:

> No matter whom we fall in love with, we sooner or later fall out of love if the relationship continues long enough. This is not to say that we invariably cease loving the person with whom we fell in love. But it is to say that the feeling of ecstatic lovingness that characterizes the experience of falling in love always passes. The honeymoon always ends. The bloom of romance always fades.[4]

Vronsky, from our earlier example, was experiencing the loss of that "feeling of ecstatic lovingness." Because he had chosen to always live within the realm of the ecstatic, he was not satisfied with anything else. Therefore, "he began to clutch at every passing caprice" to strive for that one love which would satisfy his questing heart.

Like Vronsky, many of us also fail to understand love. It is an experience upon which we foist all our unmet needs and from which we long to emerge forever refreshed, renewed, and revitalized. Dr. Peck says that "the experience of falling in love probably must have as one of its characteristics the illusion that the experience will last forever." When we sense the honeymoon is over and the bloom is faded, the assumption so frequently made is "I guess I made a mistake; I'm no longer in love."

I am not suggesting that we cease striving altogether. Searching for persons who contribute to our emotional development, striving to better ourselves through personal development, and seeking to grow professionally are legitimate quests and important to our self-actualization. I'm currently striving toward the completion of a new professional goal. I'm enrolled in the Graduate Psychology Department at Pepperdine University with the intention of earning a master's degree in psychology and a marriage, family and child counselor license. Within a few years, I plan to be in private practice. This career change is simply because after ten years at Biola, I'm eager for new vistas and challenges, eager to fulfill a longheld ambition.

Pursuing new experiences and achievements is exhilarating and healthy. But in each of the arenas we've discussed there's the possibility of blind striving, an inability to see the limitations of that for which we strive. Many of us are slow to learn the obvious. We continually fall into the trap of thinking, *If I just had . . . I would be much more content.* Possessions and life itself have meaning only when I come to terms with the God who created all things. When he is my foundation, the Being around whom my life revolves, only then will I have a sense of purpose. When that purpose becomes well defined, I recognize that everything I strive for is limited in its potential to produce fulfillment. That does not mean I can't, shouldn't, or won't seek after those experiences we've discussed in this chapter. But it does mean I must realize that my ultimate joy will never come from things or persons. It will only come from a personal knowledge of and commitment to God.

In the midst of all his resplendent living, the writer of Ecclesiastes concludes: "I know that everything God does will remain forever; there is nothing to add to it and there is nothing to take from it" (3:14). The lack of permanence so common to the affairs of the heart directly contrasts with the longevity of the love we receive from God. We experience the joy that "would fill the earth and last till the end of time" only as we commune with the divine. "Everything God does will remain forever."

A number of years ago, when I was teaching several women's Bible studies a week, a woman came to the Monday morning study at the encouragement of her neighbor. It was obvious that she would rather be anywhere but in that group. Tension lined her face—I was sure once she was able to make her escape she'd never return. To my amazement, she was back the next week. This time she didn't look ready to bolt out the door, although she still didn't look relaxed about being there. The weeks passed and this woman continued to attend the study. I was thrilled when she invited me to her home for lunch. She had been an enigma to me because, though she was pleasant, she was relatively uncommunicative with everyone.

As I sat in her palatial living room looking over a spacious backyard complete with swimming pool and tennis court, she began to tell me about her life. She was married to a businessman so consumed with his work he was rarely home. Their two children were in college. She had three expensive cars in the garage, diamonds, exotic vacations—everything she wanted. But she still wasn't content. She wanted more but didn't know what it was she wanted. Her husband couldn't understand her growing moodiness and increasing dependence on Valium.

Over the weeks that followed, my new friend came to realize her possessions were not empty, she herself was empty. Her possessions could only have meaning if she did. Ultimately she filled that seemingly insatiable void with the Giver of all good things, Christ Jesus, who said, "I came that they might have life, and might have it abundantly" (John 10:10).

In the twelve years that I have known her, wonderful transformations have occurred. Not only has the look of tension disappeared from her face, but she is one of the wittiest people I know. Some of my greatest laughs have come as a result of her well-timed comments. (Those comments are usually made as she beats me soundly at tennis each week!) When I first met her, I would never

Choosing the Amusing

have guessed she could be the life of the party, but she is now. What happened? She recognizes that it is God who gives meaning to her and her life; she is released to abundant living. That abundant living includes not only the balanced enjoyment of possessions, but an altering of perspective that brings joy and allows humor and laughter to bubble to the surface.

When we learn to enjoy life free of blind strivings, we relax; we smile; we laugh. We can see the limitation of that for which we strive—we put it all in perspective. When we achieve, we're glad; when we acquire, we enjoy; but we do so remembering the Source of that enjoyment.

Developing a Laugh Lifestyle

The ability to laugh, to see humor in the events that surround us, has nothing to do with the ability to create humor. As I said in chapter 1, few of us are gifted with a wit capable of producing convulsive laughter, but we are all capable of appreciating and responding to humor. It is a gift God has bestowed upon each of us. But that gift is frequently unused because we feel a certain seriousness and decorum must characterize our lives as adults. Leo Buscaglia makes some interesting comments about this subject.

Many people persist in suppressing the spirit of joy, in the unfortunate belief that life is strictly serious business. We often view silliness or childishness as regressions in behavior instead of realizing that each of us has a ridiculous side and that the child in us is one of our most prized possessions. We cultivate refinement and sophistication at the expense of spontaneity and fun. Polite tittering substitutes for unrestrained laughter. Joyous impulses are moderated or lost altogether in deference to common sense or good taste.[1]

Buscaglia claims "the child in us is one of our most prized possessions." I couldn't agree more, and yet, I wonder how many people recognize that dimension of themselves as being valuable—a prized possession. I am not going to suggest a technique by which we can learn to laugh with greater frequency. Our ability to laugh depends on our attitude, not on a method. One of the sources of that attitude is the child-spirit that exists within all of us. It may be lying dormant or repressed, but it is there. Let me give you an example of the unrepressed child-spirit.

For several years, Ken, Jeff, Beth, and I rented a little house on the water's edge on Balboa Pennisula. We would stay there for a week in the month of July, thoroughly enjoying the water, the sun, watching the sailboats, and playing in the sand. During one of our stays there, Ken had to leave for an evening board meeting and planned to be gone for a number of hours. Since Beth and Jeff had each established social ties with children several houses away, I invited Luci Swindoll to come down for the evening to keep me out of mischief.

We sat on the end of the boat dock listening to the rhythmic slapping of the water on the sand beneath us, watching the sailboats languidly make their way back to their place of mooring. As the sun slipped behind the skyline, Luci unexpectedly jumped to her feet. "Marilyn! Who owns that little dinghy tied to the end of this dock? Come on. Let's get in it and row across the bay." Now I had spent several hours just that afternoon watching what appeared to be every kid in Southern California repeatedly capsize that dinghy. My sense of self-preservation came to the fore, and I told Luci there was no way I'd get in that dinghy! For one thing there wasn't room for two persons and I had noticed that with even one person in it, the boat seemed to be upside down with far greater frequency than rightside up. Not only that, it was not our dinghy and we had no right to take it. Ignoring my protestations, she dashed about looking for the oars. Finding only one, she convinced me her years of summer living on Carancahua Bay taught her naval competence, and that if we sat still, we could both fit in the dinghy and even make it across the bay with one oar. I don't know why I listened to her, but the next thing I knew, we were sitting knee to knee in that tiny little dinghy, zigzagging our way into the middle of the bay.

It took only a few minutes for me to get into the spirit of this crazy adventure. The moon was rising, the air was invigorating with that slight penetrating dampness I love in a beach night. The receding lights from the shoreline twinkled cheerfully. As we lurched farther and farther into the middle of the bay, I became increasingly giggly over the ridiculousness of Luci's one-oared rowing that necessitated a constant wide-arched swing of the dripping oar over our heads as she switched from left to right. Thinking how nutty we would look to anyone watching, I was glad for the darkness and the anonymity it provided. Suddenly and without warning, we were illuminated by a bright light.

An amplified voice from a harbor patrol boat filled the air and demanded to know why we were on the water without a light. I felt compelled to confess we had no light and we only had one oar. Luci intercepted my confession with a shouted acknowledgment to the patrol that we were indeed without a light and that we would make our way to shore immediately. Drenched in the blinding glare of the spotlight, we made our uncertain way to someone's boat dock. Only as we pulled our cramped bodies out of the dinghy and hoisted it out of the water did the searchlight snap off. As the harbor patrol boat moved on past us, the amplified voice, with the faintly discernible sounds of muffled laughter in the background, said simply, "Good night, ladies."

Sometime later I was relating that incident to a group of people. A quasi-friend sitting next to me reached over and, with condescending sweetness, patted my hand and said, "Marilyn, when are you ever going to grow up?" I gave her one of my better moronic smiles and made no attempt to answer her question. Obviously, this woman assumed my experience evidenced the kind of "childishness and regressive behavior" Buscaglia claims many people try to avoid.

What constitutes regressive behavior, silliness, or childishness? Admittedly, there is nothing more tragic than an adult who fails to gain the maturity and wisdom necessary to live a responsible and productive life. But it is equally tragic when adults forget how to give vent to their "play instincts" and live out their days with such seriousness that they die having existed in a state of emotional rigor mortis.

As in all arenas of successful living, we attempt to work toward a balance. The Danish philosopher Soren Kierkegaard maintains that what we want to remember in living is that "we all possess a child-like quality, but we do not want to be possessed with that quality." To give heedless expression to our childlike impulses is no more desirable than to suppress them totally. Kierkegaard also says that "only the mature person knows what it is to be a child." Without maturity a person does not recognize his ability to function effectively in the adult world. That person's underdevelopment is often an unrecognized handicap. The mature person, however, is able to recognize the distinction between the two worlds and can choose wisely which world to appropriate for the moment.

It is interesting that Jesus said it is impossible to enter the Kingdom unless we become as little children (Mark

10:15). I believe he recognized the need for adults to be jolted out of their dull, wooden mind-sets and assume the trusting unpretentiousness so characteristic of a child. Jesus placed a very high premium upon that childlike quality. The most profound truth in the universe is that God loves me; yet many miss that truth because of its simplicity. When Jesus said, "I praise thee, O Father, Lord of heaven and earth, that Thou didst hide these things from the wise and intelligent and didst reveal them to babes" (Matthew 11:25), he once again reminds us of how preferable it is at times to be childlike.

In addition to childlike faith, Scripture addresses and humorously illustrates the unrestricted imaginations of the child-mind. For these insights about Jesus' teaching style, I am indebted to Elton Trueblood's book, *The Humor of Christ*. Trueblood relates an instance when he was reading a portion of the seventh chapter of Matthew to his four-year-old son:

> Suddenly the little boy began to laugh. He laughed because he saw how preposterous it would be for a man to be so deeply concerned about a speck in another person's eye, that he was unconscious of the fact his own eye had a beam in it. Because the child understood perfectly that the human eye is not large enough to have a beam in it, the very idea struck him as ludicrous.[2]

His child-mind allowed the boy to perceive the message of Jesus clearly. It *is* ludicrous that we can be so concerned with the sins of others that we are blind to the prominence of our own.

There is a whimsical quality in the Matthew 23 passage about the Pharisee swallowing a camel but straining out a gnat. (The straining had to do with the elaborate cleansing operation the Pharisees went through before drinking from their cups.) They'd strain out a gnat, but never seem to notice the hairy, humpy camel pass down their throats. This is a wonderfully unique and amusing illustration by which Jesus pointed out the inconsistencies and hypocrisies of the Pharisees. That image appeals to the child-mind far more quickly than it does to the adult-mind. Christ knew how calloused adults can become and frequently used deliberate exaggeration— even shock—to startle his listeners into considering his message.

Is there not tremendous exaggeration as well as delicious humor in the image of a camel huffing and puffing his way through the eye of a needle? Jesus said that was easier to accomplish than for a rich man to give up his wealth and follow Christ. To the child-spirit that image flashes on the screen of the mind and amuses and also convicts. Because it is unique, the image becomes unforgettable. But there are those stodgy Bible commentators who have tried to explain away this image and say Jesus did not mean the eye of a needle used for sewing; they say he meant a gate in Jerusalem that was so low that a camel could get under it only by tremendous perseverance and a fixed determination. I believe Jesus meant exactly what he said. Jesus had a revolutionary message to give, and that message needed to be communicated in revolutionary as well as unforgettable words and images. The adult-mind, so programmed to translate words and experience to the probable and practical, often misses the dramatic and the delightful. The British writer Anais Nin says, "We don't see things as they are, we see them as we are." Jesus used every means possible to alter our perceptions in order that we might see beyond the rigidity of the "as we are."

The expression of our child-spirit is not limited to our play instincts. It is also in an enjoyment and appreciation of the simple things in life. I call this my "shoe-string" philosophy. I developed this perspective when I was four years old. My father had just administered a spanking meant to cure me of my wicked ways. At the conclusion of that discipline, Dad asked me what I thought about my spanking. My response to him was to announce that I didn't care because I had new shoe-strings. (They had been purchased for me the day before.) One must admit there is something pathetic about a child whose only comfort for the moment is a pair of new shoestrings. Nonetheless, a bit of wisdom is found here. You have probably noticed that a child is frequently much more content with a simple toy than one that is elaborate in its many mechanical capabilities.

The German writer Hermann Hesse wrote an essay entitled "On Little Joys." In it he gives this excellent advice:

> Seek out each day as many as possible of the small joys.... It is the small joys that are granted us for recreation, for daily relief and disburdenment.... There are a thousand tiny things from which one can weave a bright necklace of little pleasure for one's life.[3]

What are the tiny joys from which you can "weave a bright necklace of pleasure?" For me there is always that which appeals to my senses. There are certain smells which invariably put me into orbit: fresh cut grass, lilacs in the spring, roses, the earth after a rain, mountain air, fresh baked bread, Ken's aftershave. On the more peculiar side, I love the smell of gasoline, new rubber tires, basements, and—can you believe?—the mortar between bricks or stones. We have a large stone fireplace in our home and rare is the day I don't press my nose to the mortar and inhale ecstatically; it's especially rewarding just prior to or during a rain! (I can't believe I'm admitting to that peculiarity in print!) Then there is the joy of seeing the glory of nature—the sky, a tree, the ocean, a flower, the Colorado Rocky Mountains. There is the joy of feeling the smoothness of pebbles washed clean by the repeated pounding of the surf; the velvet softness of our cocker spaniel; the coolness of satin sheets against bare skin; or the coarseness of corduroy between the fingers.

One of my favorite sensations comes from drinking tea from a china cup I inherited from my grandmother's collection. It is French Haviland china and more than one hundred years old. It is so thin, so exquisitely delicate, that if I hold it to the light, it is possible to see shadows of the images beyond it. The feel of that china against my lips reminds me again of my yet unbegun campaign for the outlawing of Styrofoam cups. Life must never become so utilitarian, so lacking in gentility that we become a society content to drink our beverages from Styrofoam containers!

These are just a few examples of the many little joys within the borders of my shoestring philosophy. I'm sure you could add many more to this short list of little pleasures that guarantee an occasional squiggle of enjoyment.

A number of years ago I was indulging in one of my favorite taste treats at a small sandwich shop that also specializes in varieties of yogurt. One of my favorites is peanut butter yogurt. Now that may not sound very appealing to you, but listen to this! I slather the yogurt with raspberry topping made from frozen raspberries, and then top it off with a generous sprinkling of chopped peanuts. I was just settling my spoon into this wonderful concoction late one morning, when the door of the shop opened suddenly and a tiny, elderly lady burst through it. She scanned the shop for a second and then darted over to my table, pulled out the chair across from me, and sat down. Before I had quite grasped what was happening, she leaned across the table and whispered, "Is anyone following me?" I looked suspiciously behind her and out into the parking lot from which she had emerged and whispered back, "No—there's no one in sight." "Good," she said, and with that she slipped out her teeth, snapped open her purse, and dropped the teeth into its depths.

Throughout this unexpected scene my spoon had remained frozen between my dish and my mouth. Galvanized into action by the melting of my yogurt, I put the spoon in my mouth; the little lady fixed her eyes upon my spoon and then upon my dish. I asked if she had ever eaten peanut butter yogurt with raspberry sauce. Without ever looking at me, she said that she had wanted to try it all her life but never had. I calculated that "all her life" was probably some eighty to eighty-five years. That seemed a long time to live without peanut butter yogurt. I asked her if she'd like me to get her some. Without a moment's hesitation, she said yes but still never took her eyes off my yogurt. By the time I returned to our table with her order, she was nearly halfway through my dish of yogurt! I found this amusing, especially since she offered no apology or explanation for taking my food. I started eating what would have been hers and we slurped our way along in companionable silence.

Across the street from where we were eating is an establishment for senior citizens that ranges in care for those in fairly good health but need watching, to those in poor health needing constant attention. I classified my little eating companion as an escapee from this home. The minute she finished her yogurt, she began rapid preparations to leave. She whisked her teeth out from the bottom of her purse, popped them in place, and jumped up, heading for the door. Concerned about her crossing the busy intersection alone, I asked if she'd let me accompany her. She was out the door and into the parking lot so fast I had to almost run to keep up with her. She never granted permission for me to go with her, but I trotted along anyway. As I had surmised, she made her way into the senior citizen's building and scurried down the hall. The only thing she said to me was that she had to hurry or she'd miss lunch.

I stopped at the nurses' station and asked the girl behind the counter if she had noticed the little lady I had come with. She said, "Oh yes. That's Felisha; she's a real live wire." Then she asked if I happened to be a relative. I told her Felisha and I had just met at the sandwich shop less than an hour ago. The girl's eyes sparkled as she asked, "Did you by any chance buy her a dish of peanut butter yogurt?" I was a bit startled as I admitted I had. The girl laughed and told me Felisha knew every trick in the book.

As I walked back to my car, my admiration for Felisha grew with each step. What a deal she had going for her. Who wouldn't succumb to the plight of a little, elderly refugee from a retirement home who had always wanted to taste peanut butter yogurt but had never been given the opportunity? Several weeks later I went to ask Felisha if she'd go with me to get some yogurt. When I asked for the location of her room, the girl at the desk informed me that Felisha had died in her sleep several nights before. At first I felt a deep pang of remorse as I visualized that energetic lady and the short but delightful interaction I had experienced with her. However, as I crawled into my Fiat to leave, that remorse gave way to a strong feeling of elation. What a way to go. Not only did she have the enviable experience of drifting quietly from this world, but right up to the end, she entered into the simple joys in life—simple joys like peanut butter yogurt slathered in raspberry sauce, smothered with chopped peanuts and paid for by someone else.

I am making a plea in this chapter that we validate the child-spirit living within each one of us. This validation releases us from many of the pretensions of adult living. It fosters an enjoyment, even a luxuriating in the small joys of life that never cease to be available to us daily. I am also suggesting that the release of this spirit is the first step in adopting a more active laugh lifestyle. A child laughs spontaneously and wholeheartedly because he has not yet been indoctrinated by what the adult world considers subjects fit for laughter. After we have whittled away some of the deadwood of conventionality, we can investigate those little joys and those unrestrained experiences that may bring a smile to our lips. Those little joys and those unrestrained experiences vary from person to person. You may not be amused by bobbing about in a little dinghy without a light. You may not get a kick out of a dish of peanut butter yogurt. That's all right. But find out what does amuse you, what gives you squiggles, and then enter into it with unrestrained enthusiasm. You'll be amazed at the readiness with which you begin to laugh— and the frequency.

In discussing the adoption of a more active laugh lifestyle, I am deliberately not including a recommended list of joke books, funny records, television shows, or movies. They have their place and can certainly provide wonderful times of laughter. But the humor they inspire is external to who we are. The development of a laugh attitude begins internally. It begins with a foundation that is God-inspired and God-constructed. That foundation gives us security as we stand confidently on the strength of God's incomparable love for each of us. The knowledge of that foundation then leads to personal rest and divine security. Without this internal peace, the laughter inspired by all the comics in the world will ultimately die in the wind, leaving the restless void still tangible, still waiting for the next joke.

Of all people on this earth, it is those who know Christ personally who have reason for joy—cause for laughter. It is Christianity that fills our deepest need because it encourages us to concentrate on joys that do not pass away rather than those hurts confined only to the experiences of this life. In the words of Elton Trueblood:

The Christian is joyful, not because he is blind to injustice and suffering, but because he is convinced that these, in the light of the divine sovereignty, are never ultimate. He is convinced that the unshakable purpose is the divine rule to things, whether of heaven or earth. Though he can be sad and is oft perplexed, he is never really worried. The humor of the Christian is not a way of denying the tears, but rather a way of affirming something which is deeper than tears.[4]

Notes

Chapter 1

1. Leo Buscaglia, "No One Ever Laughs Anymore," *Los Angeles Times*, April 15,1984, 2.

Chapter 2

1. From *If I Ran the Zoo* by Dr. Seuss. TM and copyright © 1950 and renewed 1978 by Dr. Seuss Enterprises, L. P. Reprinted by permission of Random House, Inc.
2. *Readers' Digest*, April 1984, 62.
3. "From Star-Struck to Stardom," *Los Angeles Times*, 3 September 1984, sec. 5, 1.

Chapter 4

1. Eugene Peterson, *A Long Obedience in the Same Direction*, (Chicago: Intervarsity Press), 1980, 96.

Chapter 5

1. Paul Tournier, *The Meaning of Persons*, (New York: Harper and Row), 1957, 184.

Chapter 7

1. Reprinted with permission of Charles Scribner's Sons, from *The Children of the Night*, by Edwin Arlington Robinson.

2. Carl Rogers, *On Becoming Persons*, (Boston: Houghton Mifflin), 1961, 108.

Chapter 8

1. David Seamonds, *Healing for Damaged Emotions*, (Wheaton: Victor Books), 1981, 105.

2. Langston Hughes, "Dream Deferred" from *Collected Poems* (New York: Alfred A. Knopf, Inc.) 1994. Reprinted with permission of Alfred A. Knopf, Inc. Reprinted by permission of Harold Ober Associates Incorporated. Copyright ©1994 by the Estate of Langston Hughes.

3. Theodore Isaac Rubin, *The Angry Book*, (New York: Collier Books), 1969, 185.

Chapter 9

1. John Bartlett, *Familiar Quotations*, ed. Emily Morison Beck, (Boston: Little, Brown and Company), 1968, 715.

2. Quoted in Edward Garnett, *Tolstoy—His Life and Writing*, (New York: Haskell House Publishers Ltd.), 1974, 55.

3. Leo Tolstoy, *Anna Karenina*, (New York: Nelson Doubleday, Inc., n.d., 423.

4. Scott Peck, *The Road Less Traveled*, (New York: Simon and Schuster), 1978, 84,85.

Developing a Laugh Lifestyle

1. Leo Buscaglia, "No One Ever Laughs Anymore," *Los Angeles Times* April 15, 1984, 2.

2. Elton Trueblood, *The Humor of Christ* (New York: Harper and Row), 1964, 9.

3. Hermann Hesse, *My Belief: Essays on Life and Art* (New York: Farrar, Straus and Giroux), 1974, 10.

4. Trueblood, 32.